Indian Paintings and Drawings
from
the collection of Howard Hodgkin

Cat no. 38

Indian Paintings and Drawings

from

the collection of Howard Hodgkin

Andrew Topsfield   Milo Cleveland Beach

British Museum Press

Front cover illustration: Maharaja Bhupat Pal of Basohli smoking. Cat. no. 28.
Back cover illustration: Illumination in the form of a vase. Cat. no. 8.

First published in the United States in 1991
by Thames and Hudson Inc., 500 Fifth Avenue, New York 10110
First published in Great Britain in 1992
by Thames and Hudson Limited, London

Reprinted 1994 for Howard Hodgkin by British Museum Press, 46 Bloomsbury Street, London WC1B 3QQ

Catalogue designed by Gordon House
Typeset by The Printed Word Limited
Printed and Bound by Lecturis BV, Eindhoven, Holland

Contents

Warmest thanks to Milo Beach and Andrew Topsfield for writing the catalogue; to Gordon House for designing it and to Peter Malone for framing the pictures.

HH

Preface

It is unusual for a successful painter to be as dedicated a collector as Howard Hodgkin of an altogether different type of painting. Progressively refined over a period of more than thirty years, his collection of Indian pictures is neither exceptionally large nor comprehensive, compared to other private collections. But it is undoubtedly one of the most individual and visually exciting. Its main strength lies in the Rajput schools, especially in those intriguing areas where the robust Rajput ethos and the imperial Mughal aesthetic overlapped and interfused. Among the most outstanding pictures is a group of the extraordinarily animated elephant and hunting scenes from the court of Kota in Rajasthan. As a whole, the collection provides an unconventional and illuminating view of the expressive powers of Indian painters.

The authors are grateful to Howard Hodgkin for his unfailing cooperation, and to a number of colleagues for their help with information or inscriptions, including Joachim Bautze, Catherine Benkaim, Rosemary Crill, Toby Falk, Robert Skelton, John D. Smith, Terence McInerney and Wheeler M. Thackston.

AT
MCB

April 1991

Notes on the collection

I decided to collect Indian paintings a long time ago. I started buying them because I thought they were beautiful. Most definitions of collecting come down to one word – greed. But once the wanting stage has passed, usually when large amounts of money are to be spent on serious acquisitions, and the need for them distorts your life, then you make the horrible discovery that a collection has a life of its own: it makes its own demands. Once its design begins to form in your mind, things have to be acquired out of necessity, as well as passion. And that perhaps is the most dangerous and yet the most creative part of making a collection, because it's no longer obeying the dictates of the heart, or lower organs: the head intervenes as well. You can argue yourself into almost anything, when it's a question of buying another beautiful object.

Collecting Indian paintings may be particularly difficult, partly because it looks so easy: there are many Indian paintings in the world. Most of them of relatively poor quality, but some with the kind of historic, romantic or exotic connotations which make inferior paintings seem desirable. The great old collections were usually made as a result of circumstance, rather than choice. They are accumulations. Until the second half of this century there has been no von Bode of Indian painting. There have been no active, proselytising connoisseurs, apart from Coomaraswamy and in our own day the great Cary Welch.

I particularly like big pictures and don't mind if they are damaged, provided that the original character of the painting survives. The pictures are chosen according to my idea of aesthetic quality rather than other criteria. My collection has nothing to do with art history, it is entirely to do with the arbitrary inclinations of one person.

As a European, affected by European art and the history of European painting, I look at Indian pictures in that light. I like large paintings, I prefer broad, architectural compositions rather than small, finicky ones and I only enjoy illustration in the sense that it applies to Giotto – rather than to Arthur Rackham. The trouble with a lot of Indian painting, in so far as one can generalise, is that it is very small in scale – it even thinks small. There is a good reason for this: most Indian paintings were made as glorified manuscript illustrations or, later, as detached, book-scale pictures. They were kept in bundles and opened up and passed around while people were sitting about. They were meant to be held in the hand – often at a voluptuous moment, which is why there are a number of (almost universally poor) erotic Indian pictures. Perhaps they were poor because they had no need to be more than diagrammatic, when your partner was sitting next to you.

One of the great temptations for a European looking at another country's art – you see it among collectors of African artefacts for example – is to equate the artists you admire so much in your own culture with the works in another. I could look through my Indian collection and say, there is my Ingres, there is my Poussin, this is like a Seurat, this reminds me slightly of a landscape by Claude, this is my Uccello and so on. But that is obviously misleading. It's easy to make mistakes buying pictures on that basis, but very tempting.

I have collected a lot of portraits of men and of elephants. You don't find pictures of women that are actually portraits at all – there is one large picture of a girl singing (38), but it is idealised in that 'pin-up' style which one finds across the board in Indian depictions of women. But my pictures of men and of elephants are almost entirely portraits of individuals, or variations on the idea of a portrait – a subject I find fascinating. You rarely find work that, in a European sense, has been done 'directly from life' – possibly the large, Mughal profile of *Iltifat Khan* (12) was done from life, possibly not, but you find endless variations on conventions, on the accepted notion of a head of a ruler, for example, the accepted vision of what he looked like. The ruler in one case appears as a god from the Hindu Pantheon, as in the great Mandi drawing (30). The same goes for the portraits of elephants – they range from the naturalistic to the virtually iconic or symbolic.

I am, inescapably a European person looking at Indian painting, but that doesn't mean that I particularly enjoy the kind of Indian painting that apes Western painting. I don't like Company painting.

It's fairly easy to distinguish fine quality calligraphy even when you can't read it. Similarly, I have deliberately not learned about Indian iconography and have in my collection only a few pictures which are of religious subjects. When at last I see them together, I am surprised that my Indian pictures do have something in common: to some extent they do portray life as lived in India between 1570 and the mid 19th century.

I haven't deliberately collected scenes from everyday life; such scenes do not appeal to me when I look at Western painting. One of my best pictures, the large painting of the lake and its palace by Bakhta (40) includes an extraordinary collection of genre scenes. When I found it I felt I was buying a piece of India – it was like hanging a fragment of the sub-continent on my wall. I have never seen most of the activities depicted there – people in full court dress shooting waterfowl outside their palace and so on. But it is a picture of amazing actuality: people who have never been to India experience the same emotion about it that I do. This sense of nearness, of nakedness, of tangible reality, within an art form which is, on the whole, third, fourth and fifth hand is rare. On looking into the bottomless pit of Indian painting, when browsing through a pile of pictures in a large sale, you inevitably find copies of copies of copies. Real pictures, made by individual artists, are elusive. That picture of a lake palace is by the hand of the original artist. It's not a copy from his atelier, not a simplified version. It's moving to come across such authenticity, in the midst of arid acres of stylisation and stereotype.

Once you've had that experience, once you've found a picture like that, then you feel differently about looking through daunting piles of pictures or auction catalogues, knowing that where one Indian picture has been reproduced there is probably another just like it somewhere else. A sense of déjà vu makes you despair, yet you continue to turn the pages because every now and then you receive an authentic shot to the heart. Then you are off again and you buy another picture. I have decided that these little shots to the heart must cease. That won't be difficult because I admire and love the pictures in my collection. Many of them were a great struggle to buy, both emotionally and financially; there aren't many great Indian pictures around. The ones that are available are getting fewer. So the decision has been taken out of my hands: now is the time to stop.

I put the paintings in frames and hang them on the wall so that they become pictures in the Western sense. This is a distortion of the way they would have been looked at originally.

Putting Indian paintings into broad wooden frames makes them part of my life. It means they can be hung on the wall, they can be moved and handled with ease and they retain their physical safety and identity. I don't like putting pictures in mounts of cream coloured board, with a thin little linear frame round the edge, as museums tend to do. I think that distorts them all the more. They don't look like pictures to me, they look like specimens. I have experimented over the years with many different ways of framing. I like the one I use now; though I don't always get the proportions quite right.

I have been very lucky to find a picture framer, who is himself an artist, to make these frames for me. I think it's very important that paintings which people love and admire and want to have, can become part of their lives – rather than remain as objects in a museum. Many of the greatest Indian pictures *are* in museums – thank god for that, since it means I can go and see them, but I believe in private collections and I believe that pictures should have a life outside museums as well. I don't live surrounded by pictures – they are too demanding – but I like to be able to hang them up when I want to look at them.

I use strong colours in my own paintings, so people often imagine that Indian painting has had a great influence on my work. There are one or two pictures in my collection, not in this exhibition, which have very strong colour which could remotely relate to my own work; but I dislike this comparison because it is made so glibly. Indian paintings are small and painted with gouache or opaque watercolour on paper. My pictures are painted with thick oil paint on wood in bright colours. Many of the Indian pictures in my collection are not in fact very coloured. Their predominant shade is one of those beautiful beige colours, the tinted cream of Indian hand-made paper.

Anyway, my own pictures are totally different in subject matter – even when they are portraits. If there *has* been any influence it would be more subtle and oblique and more to do with India itself, as evoked in Indian paintings.

Painting in a studio alone is naturally a lonely occupation. Collecting, on the other hand, brings with it an almost automatic series of international social contacts, with dealers, scholars and occasionally with fellow collectors. The conversations that ensue (particularly with other collectors) can be illuminating, inspiring and sometimes quite extraordinarily childish – even descending to the level of 'My picture is bigger and better than your picture…'.

Among many friends who have kept me company while this collection was being formed, three names at least should be mentioned here. Robert Skelton, former Keeper of the Victoria and Albert Museum's Indian Section, with whom I first visited India; Stuart Cary Welch, now Curator of Islamic and Later Indian Art at the Harvard Art Museums, and the New York based scholar and dealer Terence McInerney have in their different ways inspired, argued and helped. I have written more about them in the Fall 1991 issue of the magazine *Asian Art*.

These pictures will be away from home for at least three years. I hope this will give me time to distance myself from them. When I started collecting it may have seemed a suitable 'something else to do', apart from painting. But this has not been the case and the passions and pressures of being a collector must stop.

Howard Hodgkin

Rajput and Mughal painting in Howard Hodgkin's collection

Among art collectors there are two extreme types, driven by differing urges. One is the scholar-collector or encyclopaedist, who pursues as far as he can the museum curator's aim of acquiring at least one example of everything in a given field. In Indian painting this approach is seen at its best in the great collection formed by the late Edwin Binney 3rd, now in the San Diego Museum. The other type of collector is the intuitive enthusiast. Though he may be widely knowledgeable, his judgements and acquisitions are informed more by individual eye and taste than by academic intellect. This distinction is of course artificial, for most collectors fall between these extremes. Nevertheless, on this crude scale Howard Hodgkin is to be found well towards the enthusiastic end of the spectrum.

For Hodgkin collecting has been as deep-seated a passion as painting, and he has been doing it almost as long. His introduction to Indian and Persian painting came from Wilfred Blunt, his art master at Eton, who had formed his own collection and in those informal days was also able to borrow pictures for exhibition from the Royal Library at Windsor Castle next door. Hodgkin himself began to collect soon after this, at a time when Indian pictures could still be had for a few shillings at Luzac's bookshop near the British Museum. But his turning-point as a collector came in early 1958, over lunch at a popular Polish restaurant in South Kensington. On that occasion Robert Skelton, the rising authority on Indian painting at the Victoria and Albert Museum, introduced him to the no less ascendant figure of Stuart Cary Welch, the inspired East Coast collector, scholar and populariser of Indian and Persian painting. Through force of example as well as his numerous writings, Welch has done more than anyone in the last thirty years to inform taste and to open eyes to those few Indian paintings, of whatever school or period, whose exceptional (or occasionally bizarre) quality sets them above the common run. Hodgkin immediately came under the spell of Welch's generous enthusiasms, though later he was to discover a more personal direction as a collector. As his friend Bruce Chatwin wrote:

> The upshot of the meeting [with Welch] was that Howard's hunting instincts were thoroughly aroused. He bought, sold and traded; he perfected the tactics of the bazaar; and for over ten years he channelled about half his creative energies into his collection.[1]

Among the earlier finds was the first of his great Kota drawings, *Two elephants fighting* (14), which he had traced to its owner, K. de B. Codrington, Professor of Indian Archaeology at London, through an illustration in a geographical magazine shown him by an aunt. A still more momentous acquisition was the early Mughal masterpiece, *Mihrdukht shooting at the ring* (1), which had belonged to the widow of an Islamic scholar in Switzerland. Some years later Hodgkin infiltrated this picture into his 'Artist's Eye' exhibition chosen from the collections of the National Gallery in London, thus slightly breaching the Eurocentricity of that institution.

If collecting Indian pictures has been almost as much a vocation for Hodgkin as his own painting, his way of going about it has also been as circuitous and as anxiously inspirational. In his studio, initial ideas and their successive versions will be sacrificially blocked out and reworked until, after a prolonged period of reassessment, the desired expression of a remembered feeling or moment is achieved. Hodgkin's collecting has likewise been anything but a straightforward process of accumulation, punctuated by the occasional removal of dross. It has rather been a remorseless process of critical

---

1. Bruce Chatwin, 'Howard Hodgkin', in *Howard Hodgkin's Indian Leaves*, Tate Gallery, London, 1982; reprinted in Chatwin's *What am I doing here*, London, 1989.

revision or *reculer pour mieux sauter*. When a masterpiece clearly declaring itself to be indispensable has come into view, other less brilliant or less expressive pictures will probably have been traded off to obtain it. Just as his own paintings may have had up to a dozen 'lives' before their completion, his collection too has undergone many metamorphoses. Over three decades this continuous effort of distillation has produced a relatively small group which epitomises Hodgkin's vision. In its way it is a creation comparable in character to his own painting. The two may even be inseparable, as Chatwin suggested:

> His collection is an essential part of his life's work. Any retrospective exhibition of Howard's own paintings would, in my opinion, be incomplete without the Indian collection hanging beside them – though having once made a purchase, he has an equally strong impulse to hide it, to lend it, or at least to get it out of his sight.

The influence of Indian pictures on the colour and forms of his work has become a commonplace of Hodgkin criticism, though a systematic comparison has yet to be made. The presentation of some two-thirds of his collection in this exhibition may perhaps encourage such a study. Yet the connections remain subtle ones, whether they are sensed in a boldly patterned colouristic passage, in the assertive contrast of a coloured border or in a psychologically charged confrontation of human figures. There is a basic difference between the traditional Indian artist, following and developing with unselfconscious clarity the pictorial language of his forebears, and the modern painter, who must find his own voice and establish his own principles. Another difference from Hodgkin's work is that Indian painters, though gifted with an instinctive colour sense, relied above all on a grammar of linear contours, defining form or enclosing discrete colour areas. This pre-eminence of line demanded an uncompromising lucidity of statement. Under the Indian sun everything is clearer, leaving little room for the equivocal modulations and pregnant obliquities of Western art.

Yet within the constraints of Mughal or Rajput tradition, the Indian painter could enjoy a huge freedom of expression. Relying on his royal patrons' awareness of pictorial convention, he could unite in a picture disparate but coherent elements: schematic (even desultory) architectural or landscape outlines, finely modelled passages of figure drawing, preciously intricate areas of floral or other flat pattern, opportunist shifts of scale and viewpoint, glowing expanses of pure colour or no colour at all. This kind of intuitive, evocative, semi-abstract approach to ostensibly narrative or portrait subjects is clearly congenial to Hodgkin the artist. Together with the cumulative experience of his frequent travels, it seems to have contributed to his liberating passage to India, providing some part of the stimulus for his own explorations – un-English in their brooding radiance – of the areas of emotional feeling, sensuality and memory.

Here, however, we are concerned with the Hodgkin collection in its own terms, as representing a personal view of later Indian painting which is both unusual and revealing. It is an avowedly unacademic view. Hodgkin has never gone in for the assiduous gap-filling of the scholar-collector, and one could not easily write a conventional history of Indian painting around his collection. Whole schools, periods and genres are missing. The cowherd god Krishna, the principal hero of later Indian painting, makes only a brief appearance (5), and there is only one example of *ragamala*, or the illustration of musical modes (29). The clearest indication of the character of the collection is given by its representation of schools. Some two-thirds of the paintings included here are Rajput, only a third Mughal or Deccani. Moreover, half of the pictures overall are from the courts of Rajasthan. Such a predominance of Rajasthani paintings is unusual in a private collection outside India, and is worth examining.

From the late 16th to the mid-18th century the most influential force in Indian painting was the imperial Mughal style and its provincial offshoots. Mughal painting had gained its earliest characteristic form under Akbar, greatest of the Mughal emperors (r.1556-1605), from a dynamic synthesis of the delicate Persian technique with more robust indigenous elements – some of Rajput origin – as well as European influences. This energetic style was refined under the aesthete Jahangir (r.1605-27) and institutionalised under Shah Jahan (r.1627-58), as a superbly naturalistic art of court portraiture and reportage. By the mid-17th century Mughal influences also had a profound effect on painting in the still independent Muslim Sultanates of the Deccan, and even more on the Hindu courts of the Rajput chiefs in Rajasthan, Central India and the Punjab Hills, many of whom had attended the imperial court or served in its armies. Successive waves of Mughal influence acting on existing regional traditions engendered an extraordinary variety of pictorial styles, which, as in the case of the Hill school of Mandi, could veer within two generations from near-Mughal refinement (15) to an autochthonous boldness of expression (30). In most cases, the best local artists of each generation succeeded in striking their own balance between the naturalistic technique of Mughal art and the poetic vision and expressive abstraction of the Rajput tradition. This interaction of two complementary ideals continued until the end of the 18th century, when Mughal power had waned and a new and alien empire was strengthening its hold on India. The latest painting included here is from the mid-l9th century court of Ram Singh of Kota (42), whose artists showed a final flamboyant flourish in the face of impending subversion by European modes of vision.

Such rich and unpredictable fusions of the Mughal and Rajput aesthetic ideals are implicit in most of the pictures in Hodgkin's collection. In their unadulterated forms, neither ideal seems to have appealed to him so much. There is little here of Mughal portraiture in its most refined period under Jahangir and Shah Jahan, or of the mannered curvilinear grace (itself developed from Mughal conventions) of the later Guler-Kangra phase of Punjab Hill painting. Hodgkin tends to favour the bold pictorial statement over the minutely exquisite or sweet. Again, however, the forceful but convention-bound simplifications of the earlier Rajput styles (including pre-Mughal manuscript illustration of the early 16th century, or the 17th century Malwa-Bundela school) are also unrepresented in the collection. Instead it reveals the constant experimental confrontation, found in the earliest Mughal painting and in Rajput painting from the mid-17th century, between naturalism and abstraction, control and spontaneity, high finish and deliberate coarseness; between elegance of line and potency of colour, shaded modelling and flat pattern, elaborate detail and empty space. Often these elements are combined in the same picture in unexpected and piquant ways.

This is why so many of Hodgkin's Mughal pictures belong to the Akbari period, before the energetic and mouvementé qualities brought by Indian artists trained in the early Rajput tradition were refined out of the imperial style and a stricter formality of composition began to set in. These early works include the great *Hamzanama* page (1), with its forceful diagonals and contrasts of pattern, and the no less vigorous elephant procession (2), also a large scale work on cloth. There are no examples of the more smoothly integrated manuscript style of the latter part of Akbar's reign. Hodgkin typically prefers the hybrid, sub-imperial Mughal style, found in manuscript series executed by artists of the second rank for noble (in some cases, Rajput) patrons at the Mughal court. With their assertive geometry and pattern-making and their pared-down dramatic action, the c.1595 *Ramayana* and 1616 *Razmnama* (4-5) represent a continuing interaction of Mughal and Rajput conceptions. A similar tendency to formal abstraction is seen in the study of a pair of orioles (6), whose rhythmic symmetry against a plain ground contrasts with the more exacting – and sometimes more prosaic – bird studies painted by the specialist artist Mansur for the amateur naturalist Jahangir. The brilliantly wrought portraiture of the Jahangiri and Shah Jahan periods is represented only by the uncommonly large and acutely observed bust study of the grandee Iltifat Khan (12). *Noblemen with musicians* (16) reveals more of the formal atmosphere of 17th century Mughal court scenes, in contrast here (as in some Rajput works) with the more restless tensions of the main carpet pattern. During the reign of the puritanical emperor Aurangzeb (1658-1707) Mughal-trained artists had been leaving the imperial service to work at provincial centres, in some cases at the permanent Mughal military camps in the Deccan; such new variations of stock themes resulted from this exodus. The majestic portrait of the imperial elephant Ganesh Gaj also belongs to this phase (11). A later and unconventional Mughal work is the large, elongated drawing of Prince 'Azam Shah's procession entering Ahmedabad in 1701 (17), with its pullulating bazaarful of background figures.

There are fewer paintings from the Deccani courts, always rarer than Mughal pictures and complementary to them in their distinctive refinement of colour and line. The efflorescent Bijapur vase design (8) is a superb flight of decorative fantasy. Most remarkable of all is *Muhammad 'Adil Shah riding an elephant* (10), also from Bijapur. While its composition derives from Mughal example (seen in (9) and (11)), the treatment is thoroughly Deccani in its subtle richness of colour and textile pattern and the restricted modelling of the darkly massive forms of the royal elephant.

More radical reinterpretations of Mughal models are found among the Rajput works which dominate the collection. Among the Rajasthani schools, Hodgkin has felt an affinity for two or three in particular. These are the major court styles of Kota and Mewar from the 17th to mid-l9th centuries, and after them, the early 18th century style at Sawar, a minor court in the Ajmer region, roughly equidistant from Kota and Mewar in geography and related to them in pictorial style.

The elephant and hunting pictures painted at Kota in the 17th and early 18th centuries are unrivalled in their energy of line and sense of mass in motion, as in the tumultuous collision of *Fighting elephants* (14). Rocky jungle landscapes with turbulent lakes and swaying bamboo clumps are also imbued with seething life, as in *Madho Singh hunting boar* and the *Elephant hunt* (35-36). Such compositions may derive originally from Mughal models and were used repeatedly by palace artists at the neighbouring courts of Bundi and Kota, either in wall-paintings or works on paper. But in the hands of a master artist they could be recreated afresh with formidable vigour. This creative impulse was retained at Kota at periods when the Udaipur and other Rajasthani styles were becoming dry or hackneyed. It survives still in the exuberant scene of Rao Ram Singh's wedding celebrations in 1851 (42).

The Maharanas of Mewar, who held court at Udaipur, were the premier Rajput chiefs in rank and dignity. They patronised painting, often lavishly, from at least the 16th century until the dissolution of the princely states after Indian Independence in 1947. As with the Kota school, Howard Hodgkin has eschewed the conventional manuscript illustrations which formed the bulk of the Mewar artists' production in the 17th and early 18th centuries. Instead he has favoured the more experimental phase at the beginning of the 18th century, when Mughal-influenced forms of portraiture were assimilated at Udaipur under the patronage of Maharana Amar Singh II (19-20). Many of the portraits of this period are in a distinctive, heavily stippled style with sparse colouring (21). Its antecedents are found in Mughal and Deccani works, which may themselves have been partly inspired by European engravings. By the time of Amar Singh's grandson, the sybaritic Jagat Singh II (r.1734-51), large and inventively detailed scenes of court life had become the norm at Udaipur (39). In the late 18th to early 19th century this tradition was rescued from stagnation by a vigorous offshoot of the Udaipur style practised by artists working for the Rawat of Deogarh, one of the leading Mewar Thakurs or barons. The most individual and accomplished of these painters were Bakhta (40), who had begun his long career at Udaipur, and his less refined but quirkishly brilliant son Chokha (41), who worked both at Deogarh and Udaipur until about 1825.

Early 18th century paintings from the small state of Sawar also rely for their effect on a strong drawing style, often with only muted or incidental colouring. In this they resemble contemporary Udaipur work, while having an affinity with Kota in the vitality of their elephant drawing (24). More than those schools, however, they employ bold compositional methods, with abrupt shifts of scale and decorative schemes more in keeping with the abstract Rajput ideal than with the Mughal sense of observed space (23, 25).

A similar tension between Mughal model and Rajput reinterpretation is seen in the equestrian portrait of Dhiraj Singh of Raghugarh, a Central Indian state abutting Bundi and Kota (18). In this unusually large picture the expanse of pale green, used in Mughal portraiture as a neutral background shade, becomes a statement in its own right, while the rhythmical lines of horse and rider assert the heroic martial qualities of the subject. The two Rajasthani versions of the Mughal jharokha (balcony window) portrait convention (25-26) reveal a superbly spare style of outline drawing, which in the Nagaur version (26) is complemented by luxuriant textile and mural patterns. Another classic Rajput adaptation of the Mughal bust portrait convention appears in the idealisation of the female form developed by Delhi-trained artists for the Rajas of Kishangarh, who were devotees of the poetic cult of Krishna and Radha (38).

There are fewer paintings in the collection from the densely clustered northern belt of Rajput courts in the Punjab Hills. Many of the classic phases of Hill painting are unrepresented, such as the barbarously magnificent early manuscript pages from Basohli or the mellifluous manner of late Guler-Kangra painting. Hodgkin's choice is again idiosyncratic, but shows similar concerns to his Rajasthani collection.

The early Mandi masterpiece of a wedding procession (15) teems with figures sharply defined with near-Mughal realism against another resonant green ground. The bazaar and its populace are engagingly observed, unlike the inanimate formal crowds of Shah Jahan's court scenes, viewed through the frigid hauteur of the imperial eye. In contrast to this is the divine image of Sadashiva (30) by a later Mandi master, in a powerful stippled drawing style showing an extraordinary quality of refined coarseness.

Two royal portraits painted at Mankot in the late 17th century show how much more full-blooded the Pahari artists' reinterpretation of Mughal portraiture could be compared with Rajasthani work of this date (27-28). The Mughal convention of a seated prince with attendants is transformed by the vibrancy and rhythm of line, colour and textile pattern, building up unexpected tensions between the presiding Raja and his diminutive hookah-wallah. Among the other Pahari pictures, the *Elephant eating from a tree* (31) and the *Fly-infested feast* (33) again reveal an experimentation with lightly tinted drawing styles on a plain ground, mingled with eccentric comic elements in their subject matter. The Siege of Lanka painting from Guler (32) is one of several partly finished pages from this famous series. Hodgkin has always taken a particular interest in unfinished work, for its unvarnished disclosure of the artist's first and most direct ideas. The undifferentiated, ominous massing of Rama's armies stands in contrast to the finished scenes in Ravana's palace, while the monkey Angada's central leap hinges the composition. *The disrobing of Draupadi* (34), either a late work of the celebrated Guler painter Nainsukh or by a close follower, depicts an episode of thwarted violence from the *Mahabharata*. Its restrained and elegant symmetries, deriving from the Mughal aesthetic, are combined with a subtly heightened realisation of the main drama, set against a red and brown-striped carpet.

This brief survey shows the limitations of the usual categories of chronology, region and style in appraising the Hodgkin collection. It may be more helpful to abandon these distinctions and to view the collection as a whole. This is something that Hodgkin himself has not had the opportunity to do until the present exhibition, because of his longstanding habit (noted by Chatwin above) of lending or storing away his pictures after acquiring them. Seen together, they register their own eloquent patterns of theme, expression and technique.

The most obvious feature of these pictures is their size. It has long been an axiom among the Indian paintings fraternity that "Howard likes big pictures". Whereas most Indian paintings on paper were made to be held easily in the hand and to be passed around in intimate gatherings of nobles or ladies, over half of the present selection are of a considerably greater and unwieldy size, those painted on cloth being the largest of all. It is no accident that Hodgkin possesses not only an outstanding page from the *Hamzanama* (1), the largest and most revolutionary manuscript painted for the Mughal court, but also examples from other outsize and innovative series, such as the page by the early Mandi master (15), another from the Siege of Lanka series (32), and, from Rajasthan, a page from the Sawar *Ramayana* (22). Other paintings from the favoured Rajasthani schools of Kota and Mewar are also, typically, of a grand size; those on cloth, such as the great Kota hunt (37) and *A court beauty* (41), are on the scale of palace wall-paintings. Several other pictures represent unusual enlargements of otherwise conventional themes, such as the Raghugarh equestrian portrait (18) or the Junia and Nagaur jharokha portraits (25-26). Size undoubtedly is part of their effect. When the artists succeed in harnessing their language to a grander scale, the impact can overwhelm. Colour areas become enhanced, their linear contours more emphatic. There is little comparison between Chokha's ebulliently rendered *Court beauty* (41) and miniature versions of the same subject on paper. However, large format works were also often still painted on the more customary miniaturist scale, and these may reveal, like *Rawat Gokul Das shooting fowl* (40), an abundance of brilliantly detailed passages requiring close and prolonged viewing.

We may note here a certain paradoxical relationship with Hodgkin's own work. While the Indian pictures tend to be larger than normal, his own easel paintings are often of a broadly similar size, which is to say distinctly small by current standards. (It need not be said they lose nothing thereby in their controlled colouristic intensity, compared with the bombastic gigantism of some contemporary work). In either case, there is an apparent convergence towards a size of picture which clearly seems intuitively right to Hodgkin: larger than miniaturist, but more intimate than most gallery art.

The question of colour also invites comment. Hodgkin himself is one of the most sensuous colourists working today, and as one would expect, many of his Indian pictures reveal exciting colour passages. Yet quite a large number are essentially brush drawings, with restricted colouring or modelling. Some, like *Raj Singh with a yogi* with its flower and bird-filled garden (24), exist on an intriguing (and happy) borderline between drawing and painting. But Hodgkin's interest in draughtsmanship is not really surprising, since this is more often than not the real test of quality in an Indian picture. Not many Indian artists ever had a faulty colour sense, at least until they discovered European pigments in the 19th century. But only a few masters at any period could draw at a level above the conventional. Drawing is the most immediate of the graphic arts; its marks expose the artist's integrity, without the dissimulation of paint. When inspiration infuses an otherwise stock subject, a startling recreation of the original feeling or perception can be achieved, as in the dramatic Kota subjects of *Madho Singh hunting boar* (35) or *Two elephants fighting* (14). It should be said that elephant studies reveal this aptitude especially clearly, which may partly explain why they are such a predilection of Hodgkin's. Throughout the ages it has been unheard of for an Indian sculptor or painter to produce an entirely lifeless elephant. They have always known how to convey a sense of the massive volumes and grace in motion of this royal animal, as well as its noble intelligence and humorous charm. Even in pedestrian works, the elephants usually have more vitality than the human figures, who stand stiffly on decorum.

A less important, but very characteristic feature of the collection is its condition. We have mentioned that unfinished work has a strong appeal for Hodgkin, for its revelation of the bare bones or rough-hewn aspect of painting. So too he has been unfastidious – or perhaps fastidious in his unfastidiousness – about the state of the pictures he has acquired. It is remarkable how many of them, though now well-conserved and surviving with their integrity intact, manifest eventful histories in their ragged borders or ancient creases and abrasions; one page is thought to have gained its scorch marks in an incendiary Maratha raid of 1815 (3). This acquired, rough-edged quality is also part of their effect.

As a group, therefore, Howard Hodgkin's collection has a coherence of its own, founded on particular thematic or technical concerns. Striking correspondences come to light between individual paintings, sometimes of different schools. There are apparent pairings, for example, between the two jharokha portraits (25-26), the Mewar hawking subjects (19, 21) or the two raja portraits from Mankot (27-28). Other, subtler interrelationships may well occur to the viewer. It may be mentioned finally that the cardinal purpose of Indian paintings such as those in the Hodgkin collection is enjoyment and delight.

Andrew Topsfield

Cat. no. 11 *(detail)*

Catalogue

1

Mihrdukht shoots her bow at the ring

From a *Hamzanama* manuscript
Opaque watercolour with gold on cotton cloth
Mughal, *c.*1562-77
67.8×52cm

The *Hamzanama* (Story of Hamza) recounts the fictional adventures of an uncle of the prophet Muhammad as he seeks to convert the world to Islam. In one of many exciting episodes, Mihrdukht, a famous archeress, decrees that she will marry any man able to equal her skill with the bow and arrow. She then performs a seemingly incomparable feat: shooting an arrow through a ring held in the beak of a gold bird placed high on a tower. The challenge – which is here demonstrated effortlessly by Mihrdukht while her attendants look on in awe – was eventually met by Hamza's son, Hamid.

The text for the *Hamzanama* was written in fourteen enormous volumes, with at least one illustration dominating each folio. These paintings were not mere embellishments to the text, they were integral to the narrative function of the manuscript. The importance of their story-telling function is suggested too by the narrative clarity of this scene, every element of which enhances or heightens the events being described. It was the first great manuscript project known from the period of the Mughal emperor Akbar (r.1556-1605), and by its combination of Persian stylistic characteristics with those of Hindu India it demonstrates the varied artistic backgrounds brought to the imperial workshops with those artists whom Akbar assembled. Here, for example, the minutely detailed descriptions of decorative architectural patterns – basic to Persian aesthetic taste – are seen alongside typically Indian figures defined by bold colours and presented in silhouettes emphasizing their active and communicative gestures.

The pages for this manuscript are of cloth, sometimes with paper glued to the surface. The procedure may have been necessary because of a lack of local expertise at this time in making paper of the required size; cloth, however, was a traditional support for paintings in India. Buddhist and Hindu temples had long been hung with images on cloth, and for itinerant village storytellers – then as now – cloth paintings were a sturdy, portable means to illustrate the tales being related.

Provenance: Sarre-Hermann Collection
Published: Glück, *Die indischen Miniaturen des Hämzä-Romanes,* Abb. 37 and p. 96; Barrett and Gray, *Painting of India,* p. 76.

MCB

2
A prince riding an elephant in procession
Mughal, c.1570
Opaque watercolour with gold on cotton cloth
34×39.8cm

Because pigment has flaked from the surface of this work, the narratively central figure – a young prince riding an elephant – is visible only through the faint preliminary underdrawing; the lines are fluid, however, and his gestures animated. His attendants, and the accompanying elephants, are also depicted with great verve. Such lively forms, varied facial expressions, and vivid colours are typical of the earliest periods of Mughal painting, before artists developed formulaic compositions to serve as models. By the end of the century, paintings suggest that such princely processions had taken on the character of carefully controlled ritual, an attitude we see continued in *Prince 'Azam Shah enters Ahmedabad* (no. 17). In this early period, however, the artist is instead intent on showing us the bustle and hubbub – the unpredictability – of a moving throng.

This is a fragment, and it has recently been proposed that the remaining portion is in the Indian Museum, Calcutta (fig. 1).[1] Similar compositions are known both in the *Hamzanama* manuscript, and on the few ruined wall-paintings remaining in the imperial palaces at Fatehpur Sikri. Presumably such large-scale illustrations on cloth (a Rajput example is published here as no. 37) were suspended in royal tent enclosures during periods of travel.[2]

Provenance: Lady Herringham Collection
Published: Gray, 'A new Mughal painting on stuff' pp. 459-61, figs. 1-2; Ashton ed., *The art of India and Pakistan*, no. 644; Barrett and Gray, *Painting of India*, p. 78; Ray, *Mughal court painting*, pp. 136-39; McInerney, *Indian painting,* no. 2; Brand and Lowry, *Akbar's India,* no. 24.

MCB

Fig. 1 A prince riding an elephant in procession (top portion).
Indian Museum, Calcutta (acc. no. 304).

1. McInerney, *Indian painting,* pp.14-17.

2. In Beach, *Early Mughal painting*, pp. 76 and figs. 55-56, the composition is compared to that of a *Hamzanama* illustration, with which it is contemporary; and fig. 57 shows a similar cloth painting suspended in a tent complex.

3
A hunter shoots a leopard
From an *Anwar-i Suhaili* manuscript
Mughal, c.1570-75
Opaque watercolour with gold on paper
13.3×17.8cm

The *Anwar-i Suhaili* (Lights of Canopus) is an adaptation and translation into Persian of the Sanskrit *Panchatantra*, a series of tales that also inspired Aesop's fables. In this particular narrative, a lynx is distressed by the viciousness of his best friend, a lion. When he observes a series of animals, each of which attacks and slays a smaller creature, to be then in turn slain by one larger, the lynx realizes that "as thou judgest, so thou shalt be judged". This then becomes the topic for a conversation with the lion.[1] In this scene the lynx, at the upper right, watches while a hunter kills a leopard, who has just killed a fox. A horseman will soon arrive to seize from the hunter the leopard's skin.

Several earlier Arabic and Persian translations and adaptations of these stories are known. This particular version was written about 1495 at the court of Sultan Husain Mirza in Herat by Husain Va'iz Kashifi (d. 1504), and it became a favourite text in the Mughal world. At least four important early illustrated Mughal versions are known: a copy dated 1571 in the School of Oriental and African Studies, University of London (MS. 10102); the book from which this page has been removed, the greater portion of which is in the Prince of Wales Museum of Western India, Bombay; a volume dated 1596-97 in the Bharat Kala Bhavan, Benares; and a version completed in 1610-11, now in the British Library (Add. 18579).[2] Of these, the Bombay copy was the most extensively illustrated. There are nine illustrations for this episode, for example, among the 231 illustrations in Bombay. As with the *Hamzanama* (no. 1), the illustrations depict moment-by-moment events of the narrative.

This particular manuscript seems to have had an especially adventurous career. According to records at the Prince of Wales Museum, their pages came from the Latifi collection, having been acquired at auction in London in 1938.[3] The manuscript had earlier belonged to the Honourable Mountstuart Elphinstone, and had been burned during an attack on his home in Poona by the Marathas in 1815. A detached sheet accompanying another dispersed page from the volume is inscribed: "saved from the fire/stone-house 1815".[4]

Provenance: Hon. Mountstuart Elphinstone

MCB

1. For the story see Eastwick (tr.), *The Anvar-i Suhaili or The Lights of Canopus*, pp. 516-22.

2. See Welch, *India*, no. 93a&b; Krishnadasa, 'A fable book for Akbar'; J.V.S. Wilkinson, *The Lights of Canopus*, for illustrations from the three dated manuscripts respectively.

3. Sotheby & Co. sale cat., 13 June 1938, lot 879, for which the description reads: "Indian Miniature Paintings, formed into an album of 2 vols., they are from two Persian MSS.; the first 44 fragments are from an Indian story of the

subjugation of demons by Solomon; the rest are fragments of a 17th Century MS. of the Anvar-i Suhay-li, Kashifi's version of the Fables of Bidpay; it is stated that the bordered pages are which they are stuck have been cut down from overs of the pages printed by the letterpress of 'Royal and Historical Bookbindings, Windsor Castle.' [sic]".

4. Fondation Custodia, *L'Inde des légendes et des réalités*, pp. 5-6. For additional pages recently sold at auction see Christie's sale catalogues, 16 June 1987, lots 124-25; 24 November 1987, lot 83.

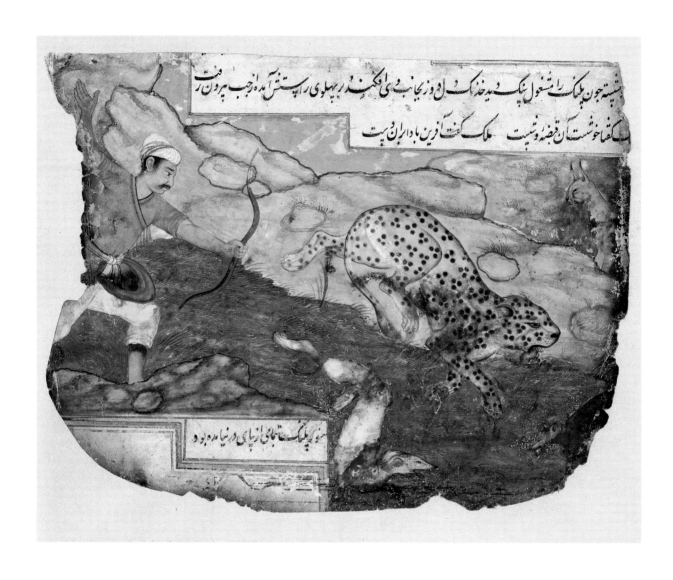

4

Rama, Lakshman and Sita in Panchavati

From a *Ramayana* manuscript
Sub-imperial Mughal, *c.*1595-1600
Opaque watercolour with gold on paper
28.8×19.1cm

The *Ramayana* (Story of Rama) is one of the greatest Indian epic texts. It describes the life and adventures of Rama, an incarnation of the Hindu god Vishnu. Banished from his homeland in Ayodhya for fourteen years, the god, accompanied by his wife Sita and his brother Lakshman, finally settled in Panchavati. There Rama asked Lakshman to build them a home:

> O Thou who are full of resource, look about on every side and
> ascertain in which spot it is fitting for us to construct our
> hermitage. Let it be in the vicinity of a pool, where the charm of
> the forest and the water adds to its beauty, where Thou, Sita and
> I, may dwell in peace, where flowers, fuel and kusha grass
> abound.[1]

The artist has depicted a far more elaborate dwelling than the simple mud and thatch house described in the text, but the strong colours and the brilliant architectural patterns provide lively visual equivalents for the physical beauty and natural abundance of the region that Rama elsewhere lauds in the epic's text.

In 1584, in an effort to make Hindu ideas more familiar to the Muslim nobility, the Emperor Akbar ordered that the *Ramayana* be translated from Sanskrit into Persian, and the illustrated imperial copy of that translation project is now in the collections of the Maharaja of Jaipur.[2] The text found on the reverse of this page, however, is in Sanskrit. The patron was thus almost certainly a Hindu noble, although the inspiration for this particular copy may still have come from Akbar's enthusiasm for the text. The character of the illustrations overall is strongly affected by the stylistic conventions of imperial court painting, although the strength of both colour and pattern that so distinguishes this illustration indicates that a strong Rajput stylistic element dominated the set – something unthinkable at this time in works from the imperial workshop.

Published: McInerney, *Indian painting*, no. 7.

MCB

1. H.P.Shastri tr., *The Ramayana of Valmiki*, II, p. 34. The identification of this episode, which corresponds to Book III, chapter 15 of the original text, was made by Terence McInerney.

2. See Das, 'An introductory note on the Emperor Akbar's *Ramayana* and its miniatures'. For further references to the series discussed here, see Chandra, 'A series of *Ramayana* paintings'; and for additional dispersed pages, see Heeramaneck, *Masterpieces of Indian painting*, pls. 197 (printed in reverse) and 198, and Beach, *The imperial image*, fig. 18, p.130.

5

The blind King Dhritarashtra embracing the statue of Bhima

By Qasim
From a *Razmnama* manuscript
Sub-imperial Mughal, c.1616-17
Opaque watercolour, ink and gold on paper
38.8×24cm
Inscribed in Persian: *'amal-i Qāsim* (work of Qasim)

The *Razmnama* is a translation into Persian of the great Sanskrit poem *Mahabharata*. The longest epic known in any language, its many-faceted narrative describes and comments on the rivalry of cousins, the Kaurava and Pandava families. The episode shown here comes at the very end, when the blind Dhritarashtra, the father of the Kauravas, attacks the Pandava Bhima. The god Krishna, realizing that Dhritarashtra would later regret his action, substituted an iron statue for Bhima; in his rage, however, the patriarch still thinks he is destroying his rival. Krishna and the living Bhima, standing to the left, watch the attack.

The translation project was initiated by the Emperor Akbar in 1582, as part of a conscious effort to make the great works of Hindu literature available to the Persian-speaking Muslim population (see also no. 4). When the translation was completed, a copy of the text illustrated by the greatest imperial painters was presented to the emperor, and according to contemporary sources, "when fairly engrossed and embellished with pictures, the Amirs had orders to take copies of it, with the blessing and favour of God."[1]

The copy of the *Razmnama* from which this page comes is now dispersed, but two pages bear a date equivalent to 1616-17. Several of the illustrations are inscribed with the artists' names; many – including Qasim – had earlier worked on a *Ramayana* manuscript belonging to 'Abdur-Rahim Khankhanan, or were otherwise known to have been in his employ.[2] This manuscript must have been made in the same workshops, perhaps also for the Khankhanan, the Commander-in-Chief of Akbar's military forces.

Published: Grube, *Islamic paintings*, no. 245.

MCB

1. 'Abd ul-Qadir ibn-i Muluk Shah, al-Bada'oni, *Muntakhab ut- Tawarikh*, pp.330-31.

2. For further discussion of these artists, see Beach, *The imperial image*, pp.128-55; and Seyller, 'Model and copy', where the two known dated pages from this volume are reproduced as figs. 1-3. Folio 346r. in the Freer *Ramayana* is by Qasim, and must have been painted at the same time as *The blind King Dhritarashtra*, with which it is stylistically identical.

6
Two Orioles
Mughal, c.1610
Opaque watercolour on paper
15.1×8.6cm

The bird at the top is the Golden Oriole (*Oriolus oriolus*), an inhabitant of deciduous forests and woods, and widespread from Europe to India. The lower bird is the Black-headed Oriole (*Oriolus xanthornus*), also frequently found in moist forest environments. Both were common to any Indian garden. The unidentified artist has taken considerable license, however; the wing and tail patterns are not technically correct.[1] Indeed, some similar illustrations show quite fancifully inventive birds.

In their memoirs, the emperors Babur and Jahangir both described carefully specific birds and plants which had attracted their interest, and illustrated copies of these texts include carefully observed studies of individual species.[2] An established tradition of bird illustrations within the Persianate world provided one model for these works, as did Chinese paintings at a later date.[3] This illustration, however, is one of a group that seems closely related to European natural history studies of the late 16th to early 17th centuries,[4] and indeed at this time European prints and books were available in quantity in Mughal territories due to the presence of European missionaries and traders. Like their European counterparts, the Mughal studies isolate birds against either blank paper or decoratively placed floral or landscape elements, and in each – as here – one bird is often attacking an insect. Works of this type are clearly a specific sub-group within Indian ornithological illustrations, and they are among the most observant and brilliantly painted of all Mughal illustrations.

Published: Spink and Son, *Indian miniature painting*, no. 2.

MCB

1. I am very grateful to Bruce Beehler, of the Smithsonian Institution, for these identifications and comments.

2. For examples drawn from two separate *Baburnama* manuscripts, see Tyulayev, *Miniatures of Babur-nama*, and Suleiman, *Miniatures of Babur-nama*.

3. See Beach, *Early Mughal painting*, pp.32-35, figs. 17-22.

4. Two additional works are in the Musée Guimet, Paris. See Bibliothèque Nationale, *A la cour du Grand Moghol*, nos. 117-18.

7
Three bamboo shoots
From a *De Materia Medica* of Dioscorides manuscript
Deccani, perhaps at Bijapur, dated 1595
Opaque watercolour on paper
40.2×27cm

The text of *De Materia Medica* discusses the medicinal properties of specific plants. Written in Greek in the first century A.D., it became a favourite text in both Europe and the Near East, and several copies of a translation into Arabic are known.[1] The copy from which this page has been removed was reportedly written in Persian, perhaps for Sultan Ibrahim 'Adil Shah II at Bijapur, and dated A.H. 1004/1595 A.D.[2]

The illustration shows two different forms of bamboo, and is meant simply to document physical appearance to allow identification. There is no conscious attempt to make a formally composed design, and in this way the page follows a format traditionally accepted for the illustration of this text but not otherwise indicative of the character of the local Bijapur artistic style (see also nos. 8 and 10). The result is exhilarating, however, with a freedom and directness found in few other illustrated copies of this text.

Published: Hodgkin and McInerney, *Indian drawing*, no. 45

MCB

1. For a discussion of these see Grube, *Muslim miniature paintings*, pp . 2-4 .

2. The provenance has been suggested by Simon Digby, as given in McInerney, *Indian Painting* p.48. For references to the literary interests of Ibrahim 'Adil Shah II, see Ibrahim 'Adil Shah, ed. N.Ahmad, *Kitab-i-Nauras*.

8
Illumination in the form of a vase
Deccani, from Bijapur, c.1600
Opaque watercolour with gold on paper
25.5×16.7cm

In the late 16th to early 17th centuries, Mughal artists excelled in depicting naturalistically descriptive forms; even flowers–those in *Two Orioles* (no. 6), for example–could be documentary portraits of specific plants. Painters in the Deccani kingdom of Bijapur, on the other hand, were seldom interested in such illusions of nature. If a natural colour could be made more intense, or the shape of a leaf more curvaceous or elegant, fidelity to nature was no constraint. This depiction of a vase is a decorative fantasy. It neither documents an existing object nor tells any story. The expressive power of its formal qualities and its technique thus assumes an unavoidable directness.

Both here and in *Sultan Muhammad 'Adil Shah of Bijapur riding an elephant* (no. 10), for example, the artists have used gold in a particularly rich and expressive way. Several tonalities of gold are placed in contrast here, and this visually interweaves the gold with the range of colour pigments to create great sumptuousness. And in both works tooling has been added: to create a design in the sultan's robe in no. 10; and to define and accentuate curves, as well as to create contrasting textures and reflectiveness, in this especially brilliant image.

MCB

9

Elephant and rider

Mughal, c.1640
Opaque watercolour with gold on paper
32×45cm

Among the earliest objects of artistic importance from India, carved seals from the Indus Valley civilization of about 1500 B.C. already show sympathetic and technically expert depictions of elephants; and later cultures, whether dominated by Buddhist, Hindu, Jain, or Muslim ideas, give great prominence and importance to images – both natural and symbolic – of this most distinctive Indian animal. It seems to have been the Mughal emperors, however, who first assembled albums of portraits of specific elephants, often accompanying these with inscriptions giving the animal's name and value, as well as its source had it been a gift. Imperial memoirs and biographies frequently remark on especially important elephants.[1] As early as 1608, the Emperor Jahangir noted that whereas the elephants of the Rajas of India had not previously been expensive, "now they are very dear".[2]

Portraits of individual elephants are known from the period of Akbar's rule.[3] During the period of Shah Jahan, these more informal depictions were replaced by a formulaic presentation in which elephant and rider(s) were carefully positioned and described, with an inscription of consistent format usually placed between the elephant's legs.[4] This suggests that the portraits were intended to provide a visual inventory of the elephant stables, or at least of the most important animals. In concept, this develops from the albums of court portraits initiated by Akbar and continued by his successors.

This image is a particularly majestic portrait. Yet while the effect is convincingly naturalistic, the use of light and shade is purely arbitrary: it is there to enhance a sense of power and volume rather than to describe the effect of light on elephant skin. However, the saddle cloth is so accurately described that it could be specifically identified, and even the texture and visual effect of the translucent robe worn by the rider is a reproduction of the physical properties of cloth. These are specifically Mughal interests (see also no. 11); a similar portrait (no. 10) from Bijapur, in the Deccan, shows quite different concerns.

Published: Pal et al., *Romance of the Taj Mahal*, p.177, fig. 189.

MCB

1. Abu'l Fazl, *'Ain-i Akbari*, I, pp.123-139, includes an extended discussion of imperial elephants, including their classification and care, and the various imperial biographies and memoirs all record events centred on specific elephants. Manucci, *Storia do Mogor*, II, pp. 337-340, lists the names of the chief elephants in the imperial stables under Aurangzeb (r.1658-707).

2. Jahangir, *Tuzuk*, I, p.140.

3. Among the earliest depictions made independent of an historical manuscript context are the portraits of an otherwise unidentified chained female elephant nursing (Christie's sale cat., 11 June 1986, lot 133); of 'Alam Guman, presented as booty captured from the Rana of Udaipur in 1614 (Jahangir, *Tuzuk-i Jahangiri*, I, pp. 259-60; illustrated in Welch, *Art of Mughal India*, no. 36); and of a small African elephant which had come from Abyssinia by ship in 1616 (Jahangir, op. cit., I, p.323; and Ehnbom, *Indian miniatures*, no. 22). See also British Museum, *Paintings from the Muslim courts of India*, no. 124; and Beach, *The art of India and Pakistan*, no. 28.

4. Among the most important examples are the following illustrations:

Portrait of Mahabir Deb. Victoria and Albert Museum (I.M. 23-1928). Published: Hodgkin and McInerney, *Indian drawings*, no. 17.

Portrait of Madhukar. By Hashim. Fitzwilliam Museum, Cambridge (PD 84-1948). Published: Hodgkin and McInerney, op. cit., no. 16.

Portrait of Madhukar Gajraj. Dated 1633-34. Staatliche Museen, Berlin (4596.9).

Portrait of Maharup (formerly named Khush Khan). Victoria and Albert Museum, London (I.M. 23-1928).

Dara Shikoh and his son on Man Murat. By Govardhan. Staatliche Museen, Berlin (4596.8).

Portrait of Sardar Gaj. By La'lchand. Formerly Kevorkian collection. Published: Martin, *Miniature paintings and painters*, II, pl. 218A.

Dara Shikoh on a white elephant. Staatliche Museen, Berlin (4596.12).

A young prince on a white elephant. Attributed to Bichitr. Private collection. Published: Beach, *Grand Mogul*, no. 33.

10

Sultan Muhammad 'Adil Shah of Bijapur and Ikhlas Khan riding an elephant
By Haidar 'Ali and Ibrahim Khan
Deccani, from Bijapur, c.1645
Opaque watercolour with gold on paper
32×44.5cm
Inscribed in Persian: *'Amal-i Haidar 'Alī va Ibrāhīm Khân* [Work of Haidar 'Ali and Ibrahim Khan].

Muhammad 'Adil Shah was the second son of Ibrahim 'Adil Shah II (r.1579-1627), the greatest of the Sultans of Bijapur and probably the most important patron of painting in the Deccan (see also no. 8). Born in 1613, Muhammad 'Adil Shah himself ruled Bijapur between 1627 and 1656, and during this period the kingdom reached its greatest physical extent, touching both coasts of the subcontinent.[1] His sister had earlier married Sultan Daniyal, the brother of the Mughal Emperor Jahangir, but despite such ties the Bijapur court remained a strong rival to the Mughals, who continually demanded subservience and tribute. Elephants were occasionally among the offerings sent from Bijapur to the imperial court. Shah Jahan's biography records such a gift in 1636:

> Makramat Khan arrived from Bijapur and had the good fortune of saluting the sublime threshold, bringing with him 'Adil Khan's [Muhammad 'Adil Shah's] tributary offering, composed of rare gems, jewelry, splendid elephants that looked like moving mountains, horses of Arab breed, and other valuables.[2]

The *Maathir-ul-Umara*, a later historical chronicle, is even more specific, naming the most important elephant, of whom portraits have survived.

> Mukramat [*sic*] Khan…in the 9th year [=1636 A.D.] returned with a tribute consisting of rareties of all kinds, and an elephant which was the finest of its species and bore the name Gajraj.[3]

And again in 1638, Shah Jahan's official chronicles record:

> In these days also, there were presented to His Majesty two elephants which Adil Khan had lately dispatched to court by way of tribute: the foremost of his male elephants, named *Maqbul-i-Shahi*, caparisoned with gold trappings and housings covered with pearls, accompanied by a female.[4]

Bijapur, therefore, was a very important source for the imperial elephant stables.[5]

The dark-skinned man riding behind the aureoled sultan in this illustration has been identified as Ikhlas Khan, an Abyssinian slave who had become prime minister.[6] (The most important precedent for such a rise to power occurs in the career of Malik Ambar, a slave who had become *de facto* ruler of the Deccani kingdom of Ahmadnagar earlier in the century.[7]) The main purpose of the painting, however, is to be a portrait of a specific elephant, rather than one of ruler and courtier – it follows such Mughal examples as *Elephant and rider* (no. 9). Similar and contemporary portraits are known as well from Rajput kingdoms,[8] further attesting to the power of Mughal artistic precedents to the styles and subjects developed elsewhere in India.

A regional stylistic character is nonetheless still evident here. In comparison with *Elephant and rider*, for example, the Deccani artists emphasize the silhouette of the animal, rather than its volume and physical weight, and the trunk and legs are arranged to create lively surface rhythms. The design of the saddle cloth is also less clinically described, and Muhammad 'Adil Shah's skirt, an opulent, dense pattern, gives little sense of the weight or texture of cloth – an aspect of great concern to his Mughal compatriot. Thus while the Mughal work catalogues the physical traits of a particular animal and its rider (and associated textiles and jewels), the Deccani portrait uses the same formula as inspiration for a brilliantly decorative design.

Published: British Museum, *Paintings from the Muslim courts of India*, no. 179; Zebrowski, 'Transformations in seventeenth century Deccani painting at Bijapur', p.177, fig. 429; idem, *Deccani painting*, pp.131-33, fig. 100, (where further information is given on the artists); Topsfield, *Introduction to Indian court painting*, pl. 17; Welch, *India: Art and culture*, no. 200.

MCB

1. Verma, *History of Bijapur*, pp.27-31.

2. 'Inayat Khan, *The Shah Jahan Nama*, eds. Begley and Desai, p. 189.

3. Shah Nawaz Khan, *Maathir-ul-Umara*, II, p.265.

4. Ibid., p.221. A portrait drawing of an elephant named Mahabir Deb (formerly known as Khush Khan), presented by Muhammad 'Adil Shah, is in the Victoria and Albert Museum (Hodgkin and McInerney, *Indian drawing*, no. 17).

5. According to an inscription on a portrait of the elephant Maharup (or Mahasarup), it too was given to the emperor by the 'Adil Shah ruler. See no. 9, note 4 for a portrait of that animal.

6. See Zebrowski, *Deccani painting*, pp.122-38, for a discussion of this period and several additional portraits of both men.

7. For biographies see Shyam, *Life and times of Malik Ambar*, and Tamaskar, *Malik Ambar*. For a more general discussion see *African presence in Early Asia*, a special issue of *Journal of African Civilizations*, VII, no. 1 (April 1985).

8. McInerney, *Indian painting*, no. 23, reproduces a slightly later example from Bikaner. A further Rajput example, *Elephant eating from a tree*, is found here as no. 31, and can be compared to a dated elephant portrait of 1609/10 in Berlin (Hickmann and Enderlein, *Indische Albumblätter*, pl. 5).

11
The elephant Ganesh Gaj and rider
Mughal, c.1660-70
Opaque watercolour, ink and gold on paper
32×48.8cm
Inscribed on the reverse: (in Persian script) *tasvīr-e fil* ("Picture of elephant"); (in devanagari and Persian scripts) *pirāg dās*[1] and *qimat 30* ("value 30")[2]; (in devanagari script, in lower left corner) *pātasyāh hāthī ganesa gaj* ("The emperor's elephant Ganesh Gaj").

The accession to the throne of the Emperor Aurangzeb (r.1658-1707) was followed by a decline of patronage for Mughal painters at the imperial level. Aurangzeb was not personally interested in the arts, and many artists consequently sought work elsewhere. The style of this powerful image derives directly from such illustrations as *Elephant and rider* (no. 9), but subtle differences – the harder line which defines the edge of the saddle cloth, or the flatter shape of the elephant's ear, for example – suggest that the painter was working away from the imperial court, possibly in the Deccan, where the permanent military camps were thronged by Mughal and Rajput nobility, or even in Rajasthan. The devanagari inscriptions on the reverse indicate that the picture was once in the collection of a Hindu (probably Rajput) owner. The floral borders surrounding the illustration imply that the page was removed from an album, where such borders were common.

The elephant's rider is evidently a Mughal prince, perhaps intended for one of the sons of Aurangzeb. The painter has manipulated the proportions of rider and elephant to heighten the size and grandeur of the animal. This is also accomplished by the vantage point and the unusually low distant horizon – a spatial device derived from European imagery. Ganesh Gaj is presented as an animal of quite extraordinary size.

MCB

TA

1. This is a Hindu name (Pairag, Virag or Bairag Das?). Robert Skelton has suggested that its proximity to the price or valuation of the picture may indicate that this person was a vendor, donor or agent for paintings, or else a valuation clerk.

2. The valuation figure is inscribed in *raqm* notation (used by merchants and clerks). A further nagari inscription and small seal or stamp have here been mutilated.

12
Portrait of Iltifat Khan
Mughal, c.1640-50
Opaque watercolour on paper
43×31.6cm
Inscribed in devanagari script: *Iltaphāt Khān Amīr Shāhjihānī* (Iltaphat Khan, an official of Shah Jahan's court).

In his memoirs, the Emperor Jahangir noted during the year 1615 that "Mirza Murad, eldest son of Mirza Rustam, on the 12th of the same month [Shahriwar] was honoured with the title Iltifat Khan."[1] Mirza Rustam, one of the most powerful nobles during the reigns of both Jahangir and Shah Jahan, married daughters to both Sultan Parviz, second son of Jahangir, and Shah Shuja', second son of Shah Jahan. Iltifat Khan himself married the daughter of 'Abdur-Rahim Khankhanan, the commander-in-chief of the Mughal armies and a noted bibliophile and patron of artists (see no. 5). Soon after his father's death in 1642, Iltifat Khan resigned from imperial service at a comparatively young age, and lived his remaining years in Patna.[2]

This is the only known portrait of Iltifat Khan, although depictions of all those family members mentioned above are known. It is an unusually powerful character study for the Shah Jahan period, made more direct by the lack of pigment; nothing here distracts the viewer from the physical impact of Iltifat's Khan's personality. This is a work of imperial calibre, and was almost certainly executed by an artist from the Emperor's workshops. It is a preparatory drawing in which the artist's careful working out of final forms is easily visible – especially in such areas as the profile, the ear, or the back of the head; and given the scale it may have been the design for a wall-painting. Such virtually life-size portraits are extremely rare at this date, but a vogue for images on this scale soon developed in the Rajput states of Rajasthan (nos. 25 and 26). That this image has a devanagari inscription, perhaps because it belonged to a Hindu owner, probably early in its career, suggests that such works were used as direct models for comparable Rajput portraits.

Published: McInerney, *Indian painting*, no. 14; Hodgkin and McInerney, *Indian drawing*, no. 7.

MCB

1. Jahangir, *Tuzuk*, I, p. 298. Iltifat and Iltaphat are alternative spellings.

2. Shah Nawaz Khan, *Maathir-ul-Umara*, II, p.247.

13
A royal hunting party
Kota or Bundi, Rajasthan, c.1630
Opaque watercolour on paper
37.5×107.2cm

Because of the large scale of the central elephant in this fragmentary drawing, the rider must certainly be a royal figure. He is shooting with bow and arrow at a lion which is attacking the elephant in defence of his young cubs, and every element of the picture heightens this encounter. Other hunters on elephants rush in from the lower right, but they are smaller in scale, thus accentuating the central attack. At the far left and right are more members of the hunting party, men on horseback who observe; it is the liveliness of the drawing, therefore, rather than action which enlivens these figures. They do not distract us from the central narrative.

Artists working for the Rajput rulers of Kota (or sometimes nearby Bundi) created particularly lively and sympathetic depictions of elephants. Unlike Mughal painters, they were seldom interested in documentary portraits of the animals, or in images stressing power and majesty (such as no. 9); nor was the elephant an excuse for opulent and novel decorative patterns (as in the Deccani portrait, no. 10). It is the energy and aliveness of the animal that is so powerfully transmitted, and for Kota artists this is best shown in scenes of hunting (nos. 36 and 37) or elephant fights (no. 14).

The thematic and stylistic inspiration for these works nonetheless comes from Mughal painting. The landscape forms here, for example, are rough equivalents to those devised in the imperial workshops, while the rock-tossing monkey at the left centre is a favourite Persian motif, often adopted by Mughal artists.

Published: Arts Council, *In the image of man*, no. 207; Doshi ed., *Pageant of Indian art*, illus. pp. 35-36; Hodgkin and McInerney, *Indian drawing*, no. 38

MCB

14
Two elephants fighting

Kota, Rajasthan, c.1670
Brush drawing, opaque watercolour on paper
34.2×69cm

> When the king makes them [the elephants] fight, the wives of
> the drivers remove their ornaments, smash their bracelets, and
> put on mourning, just as if they were widows. If their husbands
> come back alive they give a great feast, just as if newly married;
> for in these encounters and combats the drivers put their lives in
> great jeopardy.[1]

Despite the danger noted above by the Venetian traveller Niccolao Manucci, elephant fights were a frequent entertainment at court. Sir Thomas Roe, the first English Ambassador to the Mughal court, stated in 1616 that Jahangir appeared every day at noon at a window (*jharokha*) overlooking an open area by the palace walls and "sitts some howers to see the fight of Eliphants and wild beasts."[2] Rajput rulers enjoyed the same sport, and just as the Mughal emperors commissioned artists to document such scenes, so Rajput painters too found elephant combats an exciting subject. This was particularly true in the Rajasthani state of Kota, yet while the local style is recognizable and distinctive, the source of the composition and even the subject is clearly at the imperial court; a Mughal prototype of this work is known from the early 17th century (fig. 2).[3]

This unusually dynamic drawing must have been made during the reign of Rao Jagat Singh (r.1657-84), one of the most active patrons of painting at Kota. It was under his rule that many of the compositions and figural conventions found repeatedly in later works were formulated. Another version of this particular composition, datable to about 1725, for example, is in the Jagdish and Kamla Mittal Museum of Indian Art, Hyderabad.[4]

Provenance: Prof. K. de B. Codrington collection.
Published: Ashton ed., *Art of India and Pakistan*, no. 484; Beach, *Rajput painting at Bundi and Kota*, fig. 75; Welch, *Indian drawings and painted sketches*, no. 44; Hodgkin and McInerney, *Indian drawing*, no. 20; Topsfield, *Introduction to Indian court painting*, fig. 24; Cimino, *Life at court in Rajasthan*, no. 90.

MCB

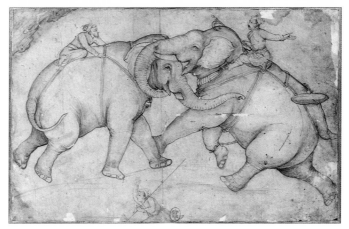

Fig. 2 Two elephants fighting.
Mughal, c.1625.
Bibliothèque Nationale, Paris
(Estampes, Res., Od 42 Pet. fol., f.30v.).

1. Manucci, *Storia do Mogor*, II, p.340.

2. Roe, *The Embassy of Sir Thomas Roe*, p.106.

3. See also Bibliothèque Nationale, *A la Cour du Grand Moghol*, no. 59.

4. Mittal, *Indian drawings: 16th-19th century*, no. 29.

15

A marriage procession in a bazaar

Mandi, Punjab Hills, mid-17th century
Opaque watercolour on paper
32×49cm

A princely bridegroom on a horse is escorted to his wedding by a procession of riders, attendants and musicians. An elephant with a royal banner precedes them, and *naqqara* drummers on camels bring up the rear. The groom wears a triple-pointed crown with a veil of pearls, and the clothes of his escort are auspiciously stained with saffron. Watched by the populace, the cavalcade passes through a prosperous bazaar. The merchandise in seven open-fronted shops is depicted in unusual detail. From the left, they are selling brass *lotas* and other vessels; *pan* (betel-leaf); sweetmeats; glass and ceramic flasks and vases; knives, daggers and sword-hilts; textiles; and grains and pulses. The procession is set against a strong apple-green ground. All the figures in the painting, including the bystanders among the houses in the foreground, are sensitively observed and are the work of the same hand.

This is the first of a sequence of three paintings. The other two, in the Benkaim collection, Beverly Hills, continue the narrative with the bridegroom's arrival at a palace, followed by the nuptial ceremonies within.[1] All three are by the same master as a dispersed group of similarly large illustrations to the *Bhagavata Purana* and the *Ramayana*, which form the earliest phase of painting at the Hill court of Mandi (for its second phase, see no. 30). Strongly based in the imperial Mughal style, they are both the earliest and some of the most impressive narrative paintings from the Punjab Hills.[2]

It is not known which story or event the three wedding scenes illustrate.[3] According to a recent interpretation, they could depict the story from the *Mahabharata* epic of the auspicious marriage of the young sage Rishyashringa to the princess Shanta, which saved their land from drought.[4] But there seems to be insufficient evidence in the pictures to bear this out conclusively.

Published: Digby, 'A corpus of "Mughal" glass', pl. III (detail); Victoria & Albert Museum, *The Indian heritage*, no. 160, col. pl. 4; Glynn, 'Early painting in Mandi', fig. 13; Bayly ed., *The Raj*, no. 26.

AT

1. Glynn, 'Early painting in Mandi', figs. 14-15.

2. Their earlier attribution to Bikaner in Rajasthan (e.g. as argued in Khandalavala, 'Two Bikaner paintings' and elsewhere) is no longer widely accepted. See also Welch, *India*, no. 268 (cat. entry by J.Mittal); Goswamy, *Essence*, nos. 183-84; Christie's New York sale cat., 3 Oct. 1990, lot 80.

3. Glynn (op. cit., pp.52-54) associates them with two known *Ramayana* illustrations, mainly on the basis of the recurrent motif of the triangular flag with cloud pattern (and, in one case, a sun). However, it may be noted that the three marriage pictures differ slightly in size from the two *Ramayana* scenes, and are of horizontal rather than vertical format. Moreover, triangular flags had become common processional paraphernalia of the Indian courts by the mid-17th century: cf. Losty, *Indian paintings in the British Library*, pl. XII; also Irwin and Hall, *Indian painted and printed fabrics*, nos. 182-83, pl. 86; Brijraj Singh, *The kingdom that was Kotah*, fig. opp. fig. 12; Bautze, 'Eine Garudastandarte aus Kota', pp.63-64, fig. 2; idem, 'Maharana Sangram Singh of Udaipur', pp.125-26 and figs.

4. I am grateful to Francis G. Hutchins for kindly providing a copy of his unpublished article, 'India's Unicorn Boy', in which he advances this idea. The son of a hermit, Rishyashringa was brought up by his father in the depths of the forest. As a youth he attained great spiritual powers. When a drought afflicted the country of Anga, the king was advised by his Brahmins to summon Rishyashringa and marry him to his daughter, and so cause the rain to return to the land. Fair maidens were sent to beguile the puzzled young ascetic, who had never seen a woman before. The marriage was duly accomplished and was followed by the long awaited rains (van Buitenen tr., *Mahabharata*, II, pp.431-41). But there is a lack of supportive detail in the three Mandi paintings – such as the evidence of a drought-stricken landscape, or of Rishyasringa's characteristic deer-horn – to confirm this interpretation of the narrative.

16
Noblemen with musicians
Mughal or Deccani, perhaps at Aurangabad, late 17th century
Opaque watercolour with gold on paper
36.2×26.7cm

This meeting between two nobles takes place on a terrace alongside a lake or river. The distant waterfront is lined with walled gardens, private pleasure grounds to which boats are ferrying visitors; each has an architecturally distinct entrance facing the water. The foreground scene is an evocative reconstruction of a reception where wine is served and musicians play. It is simultaneously both formal and relaxed.

By the later 17th century, the unique qualities of earlier paintings made for Rajput, Mughal, or Deccani patrons were no longer easily found. Social intermixture and artistic interchange had blurred distinctions, and it was costume or architectural type more frequently than artistic style that defined provenances. While the robes indicate that these men are Muslim, it is impossible to know whether the patron was a Mughal noble or from the Deccan. The artist was in any case as interested in rug patterns as in any individual portrait; the green floral forms of the rug are more active visually than any of the human figures.

MCB

17

Prince 'Azam Shah enters Ahmedabad

Mughal, c.1701
Brush drawing: opaque watercolour and gold on paper
35.9×61.9cm
Inscribed in Persian (above): *Waqtīki ṣūbadār-i Ahmadābād-i Gujarāt shuda būdand, rozī-ki ...shahr mīshudand, taṣwir-i ānwaqt ast va rish khizāb karda būdand.* (When he had become governor of Ahmedabad in Gujarat, the day he was [entering] the city – a depiction of that time, and he had dyed his beard red).

Prince Muhammad 'Azam, the third son of the Mughal Emperor Aurangzeb (r.1658-1707), was born in 1653. He served as Governor of Gujarat between 1701 and 1705, and it is his arrival in the Gujarati capital that is depicted here. According to J.N. Sarkar, "[his] love of ease and aristocratic temperament made his tenure a period of peace, if also of supineness."[1] He is known to have amassed a considerable fortune during this period, and this aided his attempt to seize the throne following his father's death in 1707. After a nominal rule of three months and ten days, he and his two sons, Bidar Bakht and Wala Jah, were killed. 'Azam Shah was himself decapitated, and his head presented to his elder brother and successor, Muhammad Mu'azzam, known also as Bahadur Shah or Shah 'Alam I (r.1707-12).

'Azam Shah is shown passing through the bazaars of Ahmedabad on a palanquin. Accompanied by the imperial party, including (at the left) an equestrian Wala Jah, he is observed from the rooftops by women and children, while some shopkeepers, beggars, holy men, and townspeople are held back by armed troops; others are ignoring him completely. Careful observation reveals turbulent activity within these throngs, yet the artist has composed them into tightly compacted units that do not intrude spatially on the imperial party. He has also provided us with an illustration that documents convincingly an historical moment.

Published: Welch, *Indian drawings and painted sketches*, no. 22; Hodgkin and McInerney, *Indian drawing*, no. 39.

MCB

1. Sarkar, *History of Aurangzib*, V, p.429.

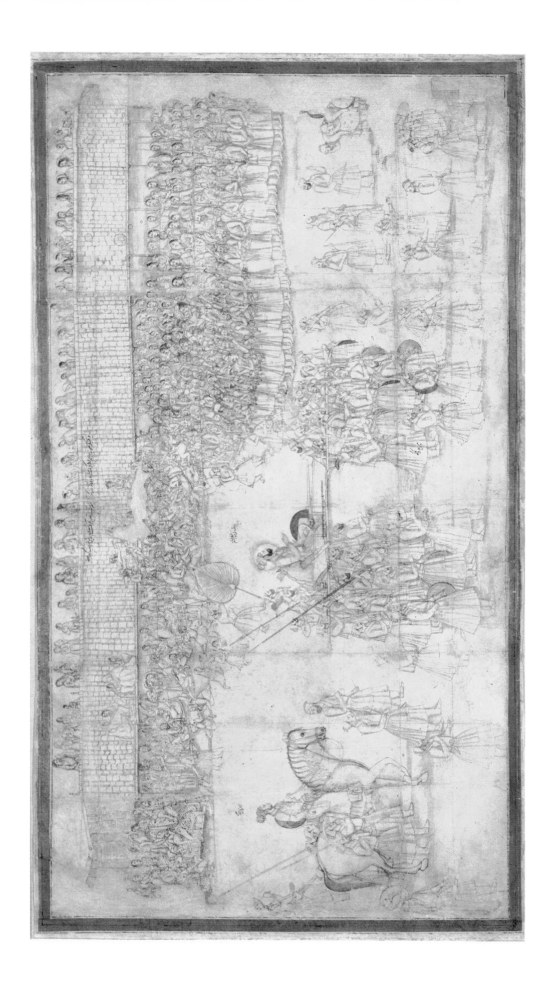

18

Maharaja Dhiraj Singh of Raghugarh riding

Raghugarh, Central India, c.1700
Opaque watercolour on paper
56×35cm
Inscribed above in devanagari script: *mahârâja śrī dhīraj siṅghjī.*

A powerful figure on a mettlesome stallion, Maharaja Dhiraj Singh rides holding a sword at his shoulder. Another sword and *katar* dagger are at his waist, close to the lion-head pommel of his saddle. His blue-grey stallion is plumed and caparisoned with dark crimson trappings. Silhouetted against a pale green ground, horse and rider massively dominate the picture area. No landscape detail intrudes, only a pair of retainers on foot, shrunk in their insignificance to trotting midgets. Such discrepancies of scale are typical of the Raghugarh painters' robust adaptation of Bundi-Kota conventions[1] to their own distinctive vision.[2] Even so, for all the accentuated rhythms of its outline and trappings, the horse also reveals the detailed observation of its Mughal antecedents, in the dappling of its cheek or the veining of its genitals.

An outlying Central Indian court to the south-east of Bundi and Kota, Raghugarh maintained its own pictorial tradition from the late 17th century onwards.[3] Its rulers were the heads of the Khichi branch of the once-mighty Chauhan Rajputs, whose earlier stronghold had been at Gagraun. The Raghugarh fort is said to have been founded by Dhiraj Singh's father, Lal Singh Khichi.[4] According to Sir John Malcolm, Dhiraj Singh was as doughty a warrior as he appears,

> …successful in all the petty wars which he waged with his neighbours. The reputation of this prince was high. The reigning Rajas of Jeypoor and Odeypoor both visited him, and each of them married one of his daughters. Dhuruj Singh was slain in an affray with the Aheer tribe, whom he had been long engaged in reducing to order.[5]

Published: Arts Council, *In the image of man*, no. 136 (not illus.).

AT

1. Cf. Bautze, 'Portrait of Jagat Singh of Kota', figs. 1-2.

2. Cf e.g. Arts Council, *In the image of man*, no. 289; Tooth and Sons, *Indian Paintings*, London, 1975, no. 4.

3. Welch, *India*, no. 251 (cat. entry by J.Mittal); Beach, *Bundi and Kota*, pp.45-48; Bautze, *Indian miniature paintings*, no. 21 and refs. A later, stylised Raghugarh subject of Rama on a horse (Pal, *Classical tradition*, no. 42; Sotheby's New York cat., 22 March 1989, lots 129-30) derives from a model similar to the present composition.

4. *Imperial Gazetter of India*, vol. 21, Oxford, 1908, s.v. Raghugarh, gives a somewhat different account, putting the construction of Raghugarh fort around 1704.

5. Malcolm, *Memoir of Central India*, I, p.464.

महाराज श्रीघ्र जसिंघज

19

Maharana Amar Singh II of Mewar hawking
Udaipur, Rajasthan, c.1700
Opaque watercolour on paper
31×43.5cm

Maharana Amar Singh II of Mewar (r.1698-1710) is seen twice, hunting crane with a hawk in open country, accompanied by attendants. On the left, his three *shikaris* (huntsmen) point out a flock of sarus cranes near a river. The royal hawk is then released and pursues the frightened flock. On the right, it brings down its kill, and the Maharana smokes a hookah held by an attendant, while the *shikaris* respectfully make their report. As is often found in earlier mythological paintings from Mewar, this continuous narrative is set against a plain-coloured background of schematic hill forms (here an unusual shade of blue), punctuated by flowering trees. In the landscape beyond, which is also divided into distinct colour areas, villagers are at work in the fields, a woman fetches water and another swings her baby.

A short-lived but innovative ruler, Amar Singh did most as a patron to introduce into Udaipur painting the genres of portraiture and court reportage which had originally been developed at the Mughal court. These were quickly assimilated to the traditional Mewar idiom. This painting shows much freshness of observation and may well be the earliest instance of the hawking theme in Mewar portraiture. It seems to predate the grisaille hawking portrait of Amar Singh in Melbourne[1] and that of Sangram Singh Ranawat (no. 21). Providing scope for both aerial and terrestrial drama, hawking subjects lent themselves well to the Mewar painters' narrative art, and larger and more elaborate versions were executed for Amar Singh's successor, Sangram Singh II.[2]

Published: Colnaghi & Co, *Indian painting*, no. 56 (not illus.).

AT

1. Topsfield, *Paintings from Rajasthan*, no. 57.

2. Ibid., nos. 78-79.

20

Maharana Amar Singh II of Mewar with his ladies

Udaipur, Rajasthan, c.1708-10
Opaque watercolour with gold on paper
40×21cm
Inscribed in devanagari script:[1] *mahārānā śrī amar saṅhajī veṭha 1/ eka jāga kesar ko cevaco nāvai/ eka jāga gulāb bāḍī luḍāvai.* ("Maharana Amar Singh is seated; in one place he is bathing in a bath of saffron; in one place he […?] the Gulab Bari (Rosewater Garden)").

From the evidence of his portraits, Amar Singh devoted himself as freely as most Rajput rulers to the secluded pleasures of the zenana.[2] He was also the first of the Mewar Ranas to take to strong liquor, following in this the example of his favourite Jaisalmer queen.[3] Here he is shown with his zenana ladies in three scenes which may represent the successive pastimes of one particular festive day.

Above, Amar Singh watches a dance performance in an arcaded hall, whose cusped arches resemble those of the recently completed Bari Mahal (or Amar Vilas) apartments of the City Palace.[4] The Rana and a nautch girl are framed in the central arch, while female musicians and attendants in a variety of costumes stand at either side. A silver door at the rear has become oxidised. In the scene below, the party has moved to a bathing-pool. Its water is stained red, as after the springtime Holi festival when coloured powder and water are liberally thrown about; however, this is at variance with the inscription, which implies that the water has been auspiciously coloured with saffron. Whether this pool is in a palace or a garden setting is uncertain. Amar Singh was fond of bathing and had a royal pool in the Sarvaritu Vilas garden, which his nobles were also privileged to use on occasion.[5] Accompanied as ever by a hookah-bearer, he stands waist deep in the pool, while the women swim or stand in respectful attitudes. Paintings of royal water-sports are known from the reigns of several later Mewar Ranas.[6]

The third scene is set in the Gulab Bari rose-garden.[7] The royal women move among the flowering bushes, gathering rose-petals on gold trays, probably for use in making rose-water (*gulab*) or in distilling the strong, clear Udaipuri liquor called *gulabi*, the feminine counterpart to the cloudy and fiery *asha*, drunk by Rajput men. Amar Singh stands with his hookah and chowry-bearers, sampling the petals offered by a lady. He wears the full beard which he adopted in the last years of his life. The days of wine and roses were not long for Amar Singh, who died in December 1710 at the age of thirty-eight.

Because of the spatial disjunction of these three episodes, the painter could not compose them in an integrated topographical framework. Instead he has adopted the old-fashioned device of superimposed registers, making possible a well-judged interplay of schematic colour areas. The blue interior of the palace apartments above is as unnaturalistic as the blue backdrop seen in the hawking picture (no. 19), but it effectively balances the red and dark brown grounds of the lower registers.

AT

1. Following conservation this inscription was reattached to the backing of the picture. Besides losing its borders, the painting has also at some time been divided and rejoined along a line between its first and second registers.

2. E.g. the garden scene in the Kanoria collection, Patna: Archer, *Indian paintings from Rajasthan*, no. 41 (not illus.), and Desai, *Life at court*, no. 73. See also Khandalavala, Chandra and Chandra, *Miniature paintings*, fig. 35; Skelton, *Indian miniatures*, no. 10; Andhare, *Chronology*, pl. 74. Several other examples are in private collections.

3. Shyamaldas, *Vir Vinod*, II, p.673.

4. Tillotson, *The Rajput palaces*, col. pl. p.111.

5. Mathur, *Feudal polity in Mewar*, p.233.

6. Two examples in the collection of the late Edwin Binney 3rd (San Diego Museum) show the aquatic revels of Rana Jagat Singh II (c.1740; unpublished) and Rana Bhim Singh (c.1810-20: Binney, *Panorama*, no. 17).

7. Cf. Topsfield, *Paintings from Rajasthan*, no. 128 for a general view of this garden.

21

Ranawat Sangram Singh hawking

Udaipur, Rajasthan, c.1708-10
Brush drawing: opaque watercolour and gold on paper
31×43.5cm
Inscribed on the back in devanagari script: *ranovat sagarām syaghjī.*

A chubby Mewar nobleman with incipient beard, identified as Sangram Singh of the Ranawat clan,[1] rides a well-groomed stallion on a hawking expedition. He is accompanied by several attendants, of somewhat smaller size than him. One marches beside him waving a chowry, others bear his arms and shield under cloth covers. A falconer with glove and bag leads the group. Another attendant gestures forwards as the hawk, seen four times in all, seizes a fowl in flight and brings it to the ground. The hilly landscape is suggested by undulating rocky outcrops with shrubs and green shading dabbed with a cloth-pad in the Mewari manner. A village and ploughman with bullocks are glimpsed in the far right corner.

The restricted palette, plain background and shaded figures are of a type found in Udaipur painting under Maharana Amar Singh II (r.1698-1710; see nos. 19-20). Over a third of his surviving portraits are executed in this sparsely coloured style with heavy stippled shading, a distinctive local version of a technique found in earlier Mughal and Deccani work. Unusually, the subject here is not the ruler himself, but a minor nobleman who sometimes appears in the royal entourage in the larger court scenes painted for Maharana Sangram Singh II (r.1710-34).[2] However, it is perhaps possible that a confusion may have arisen between the Ranawat noble and Maharana Sangram Singh himself, of whom this could be a likeness as a youthful prince soon before his accession.[3] In another, more fully bearded portrait of the same man hawking with retainers, he is followed by an attendant carrying the royal *changi* or disc-shaped parasol.[4] Both of these paintings can be related in different ways to the earlier hawking portrait of Amar Singh in Melbourne.[5] The present composition, with its statuesque central group of attendants, lacks the rhythmical movement of the latter picture, but has a wider, and subtle, colour range. It is also more varied in style, combining the sensitive drawing of the stallion, with its finely stippled head and body, with more naive or improvised touches. Its continuous narrative treatment of the hawk's kill moreover recalls that of *Maharana Amar Singh hawking* (no. 19), and the bipartite division of the hilly background is also faintly similar.

Published: Hodgkin and McInerney, *Indian drawing*, no. 34.

AT

1. A cadet branch of the ruling Sisodiya clan, the Ranawats were descended from the numerous offspring of Rana Udai Singh (1536-72) and bore the title Baba or 'infant' (Tod, *Annals and antiquities*, I, p.384). Gahlot (*Rajputane ka itihas*, pp. 343, 345-46) lists over seventy Ranawat *thikanas*, almost entirely among the third (or inferior) rank of Mewar fiefs.

2. E.g. as a mounted figure in the foreground at the Navaratri buffalo sacrifice (Topsfield, *The City Palace Museum*, no. 5), and in the Gangaur boat procession (ibid., no. 2). There he is probably the figure identified as Baba Sangram Singh, riding in a small boat with the minister Bihari Das Pancholi towards the middle of the lake. Ranawat Sangram Singh is not to be confused with Rawat Sangram Singh of Deogarh (r.1706-37), who also appears in some Udaipur durbar groups of the same period.

3. Cf. e.g. Topsfield, *Paintings from Rajasthan*, no. 58, where Prince Sangram Singh is seated sixth from the left of Rana Amar Singh.

4. Gangoly, *Exhibition of Indian paintings*, no. 243, illus. opp. p.8 (also: *Indian paintings*, Waddington Galleries Ltd., London, 1978, no. 50; Christie's sale cat., 24 April 1980, lot 196; *Indian paintings*, Tooth Paintings Ltd., London, 1980, no. 22). This painting is inscribed on the upper border: *rànavat sìgarām sìgh.*

5. Topsfield, op. cit., no. 57. Other comparable equestrian portraits of Amar Singh in the stippled style include: Skelton, *Indian miniatures*, no. 11; Welch and Beach, *Gods, thrones and peacocks*, no. 28; Sotheby's New York sale cat., 10 December 1981, lot 91; Ehnbom, *The Ehrenfeld collection*, no. 51. Another example is in the Benkaim collection, Beverly Hills.

22

Vibhishana in the camp of Rama
An illustration to the *Ramayana*
Sawar, Rajasthan, c.1700
Opaque watercolour on paper
67×45cm

Vibhishana ('the Terrifying') was the more righteous brother of Ravana, the demon king of Lanka, in the *Ramayana* epic (see also nos. 4 and 32). Ravana had abducted Rama's wife Sita and ultimately he would be defeated by Rama, Lakshman and their monkey and bear allies. Towards the beginning of the *Yuddhakanda* ('Book of the Battle'), the penultimate book of the *Ramayana*, Vibhishana failed to dissuade Ravana from fighting against Rama, and he then went over to Rama's side.[1] Eventually, after Ravana's death, Vibhishana would succeed to the throne of Lanka.

The scene is set in Rama's camp, under a starry sky. The mustachioed Vibhishana kneels respectfully before Rama, who reclines regally on a deer-skin rug at the centre of the composition, holding two arrows in his hand. His head rests on the monkey king Sugriva's lap, while Hanuman massages his feet. His half-brother Lakshman is seated behind. Rama and Lakshman, as well as Hanuman, wear the leaf skirts which they had adopted during their earlier exile in the forest.

One of the demons from Lanka is led into Rama's presence by two monkeys. This is probably Shuka, sent by Ravana in an unsuccessful attempt to undermine Sugriva's loyalty; Rama will save the demon from the angry monkeys' beatings and return him to his wicked master.[2] The members of the monkey and bear armies watch this scene, or groom themselves or sleep. They vary in size from giant mace-bearing monkeys standing sentinel at the corners of the picture to smaller and less anthropomorphic figures.

Only a few, somewhat damaged pages are known to survive from this ambitious *Ramayana* series,[3] which shows great vigour and freshness in its figure painting (especially of animals and birds) and in its compositional groupings, with bold variations of scale. Here the artist has unusually adopted a vertical composition, aligned on the central recumbent figure of Rama, rather than a horizontal one.

Published: Arts Council, *In the image of man*, no. 383 (not illus.).

AT

1. Shastri tr., *The Ramayana of Valmiki*, III, chs. 14-19.

2. Ibid., ch. 20.

3. Other pages are in the Kanoria collection (Patna) and J.P. Goenka collection (Bombay); e.g. Arts Council, *In the image of man*, no. 393 (not illus.).

23
Maharaja Raj Singh of Sawar in procession with his elephants
Brush drawing with opaque watercolour on paper
Sawar, Rajasthan, c.1710-15
52×61cm
Inscribed on the front in devanagari script: kuvās sevo[1] ("the personal attendant Sevo").

Maharaja Raj Singh of Sawar, a small state in the Ajmer region, rides in procession with his elephants, attendants and falconers. The elephants are perhaps being taken on an expedition for pasture or recreation. Raj Singh rides, holding a rose, in the howdah of the largest elephant. The attendant Sevo[2] sits behind him waving a peacock-feather fan. In front of the Raja a mounted courtier turns to offer a greeting. Attendants on adjacent elephants bear the royal parasol and a pandan (betel-leaf box), and another, on foot, carries the Raja's hookah. The human figures in the foreground are of varying scale, and some of them seem to have been an afterthought, for this is an elephant picture above all. From the skittish calves to the powerful veteran bearing the royal howdah, the fourteen elephants are drawn with a fluent and vigorous line and minimal colouring. Their progress is matched by that of the falconers and escort with the Raja's horse beyond the hill and by the royal hawks making their kill overhead.

Ajmer was an important Mughal outpost in Rajasthan, and a strong sub-imperial Mughal influence is found in the area in the 17th century, as for example in a series of Gajendramoksha paintings of c.1640, with their spirited rendering of elephants.[3] The position of Sawar, a state established in the time of the Emperor Jahangir, is particularly interesting. It is situated in the south-east corner of the Ajmer region, virtually on the borders of Amber, Bundi and Mewar. Bundi and Kota were the closest major courts, and there is some affinity between Sawar elephant drawings and those of Kota (nos. 14, 36).

A distinctive local style of painting developed at Sawar towards the end of the reign of Pratap Singh (r.1668-1705) and continued under his successor Raj Singh (r.1705-30). The local artists' use of brush drawing on plain backgrounds with limited colouring and modelling is comparable to some Udaipur work under Maharana Amar Singh (r.1698-1710); the hawking theme seen here is another feature in common (nos. 19, 21). The Sawar chiefs were themselves of the Sisodia clan and thus had close ties with the ruling family of Mewar.

Other related works include a drawing of a Raja on an elephant in the Cleveland Museum,[4] Raj Singh with a yogi in a garden (no. 24), and a large battle scene[5] in the collection of Kumar Sangram Singh at Jaipur.[6] Other, smaller portraits of Raj Singh or his father (it is not always easy to distinguish between them) are in private collections.[7]

Published: Hodgkin and McInerney, Indian drawing, no. 32.

AT

1. A damaged inscription on the reverse appears to identify the subject as Maharaja Raj Singh. Below this presumably original inscription, a later inscription on paper, of doubtful evidential value, has been attached to the back of the painting. It reads: māharāja śrī rājai sinhajī chhabī sakar ki 1713, giving what is apparently the A.D. year 1713 rather than an equivalent Vikram Samvat date.

2. Sevo is similarly identified in another painting of Raj Singh: Pasricha, 'Painting at Sawar', fig. 5.

3. Cf. e.g. Ehnbom, The Ehrenfeld collection, no. 65 and refs.

4. Leach, Indian miniature Paintings, no. 58: perhaps a portrait of Pratap Singh of Sawar. Cf. also Pasricha, op. cit., fig. 3.

5. It has been suggested that this picture represents the battle for the Mughal succession at Jajau (near Agra) in 1707.

6. It may be noted that all three of these large scale works, together with those depicting Raj Singh at worship (Pasricha, loc. cit.) and with ladies in a garden (Weber, Porträts, Abb. 110), have similar crease marks caused by folding along one or more axes.

7. E.g. Kanoria collection, Patna; and Sotheby's sale cat., 12 December 1972, lot 120 (not illus.). See also Hodgkin and McInerney, Indian drawing, no. 33: a page of artist's sketches of various subjects, including Radha and Krishna in a bower, recalling a similar finished work in the late Edwin Binney 3rd collection: Spink, Krishnamandala, fig. 68. It may be mentioned that the latter painting contains the distinctive white on brown floral carpet, regarded by Pasricha – perhaps too exclusively – as a diagnostic feature of the closely related school of Isarda: Pasricha, op. cit., pp. 265f.

24
Maharaja Raj Singh of Sawar with a yogi in a garden

Brush drawing, opaque watercolour on paper
Sawar, Rajasthan, 1714
48×53cm

Inscribed on the reverse (partly obscured by repairs): *mahārāja śrī rāj si*[*ṅhajī*] (in another hand:) [*rāja*]*sthān sāvar kā chhe*; (below:) *saṁ 1771 chhabī dīvālī par najar kī dī.* ("Maharaja Raj Singh...It is from Sawar in [Raja]sthan...The picture was presented at the Diwali festival in V.S. 1771").

Maharaja Raj Singh sits smoking a hookah on a low throne on a garden terrace. He is conversing with a visiting yogi, a smaller figure also seated with a hookah in a creeper-festooned pavilion with sloping *bangla* eaves. Dishes and blue and white flasks[1] and cups stand before him and in the niches overhead. In front of the Raja a small child plays with a rattle among the pigeons, while behind him stand attendants bearing a peacock fan, wine, *pan* boxes and his sword. The yogi has long finger-nails and beard and wears a loincloth and striped cloak. He is attended by a maid with a peacock fan and by a disciple, also smoking a hookah, together with three noblemen and an official with a staff. The formal garden, with its square plots, fountain, cypresses and flowering trees, teems with a multitude of peacocks, parrots, hoopoes and other colourful birds. In the foreground, groups of male and female musicians, separated by plantains and a diminutive pair of fighting elephants (probably a sculptural group), complete this virtually symmetrical composition.

This painting was presented by its artist on the occasion of the autumnal Diwali festival in 1714. The garden shown may well be the Raj Bagh, laid out by Raj Singh himself.[2] Combining the formality of a court occasion with the naively exuberant decorative detail of the bird-filled garden, this is a painting of unusual charm. In its playfully archaic use of rectangular compartmentation, it achieves a more integrated composition than the probably earlier garden scene in Berlin,[3] which is more naturalistically treated and shows stronger affinities with Udaipur painting under Maharana Amar Singh. Another related painting of Raj Singh in a bird-filled garden with a band of female musicians is in an American private collection.[4] Birds and music seem to have been of particular importance to Raj Singh, who was himself a trained singer.[5]

Published: S. Singh, *Catalogue*, no. 88 (not illus.); Hodgkin and McInerney, *Indian drawing*, no. 42.

AT

1. Raj Singh's hookah also rests on a blue and white dish. Blue and white hookahs and vessels are often seen in portraits of Raj Singh and his ladies, e.g. in a similar seated study of Raj Singh smoking a hookah in the Kanoria collection, Patna, and in a study of a lady with two maids on a terrace in the same collection (cf. also Sharma, *Indian miniature painting*, no. 75, pl. 73).

2. Mathur, *Brij bavani*, p.11. (I am grateful to Mr Indar Pasricha for providing a copy of this booklet.)

3. Weber, *Porträts*, pp.535-40, Abb. 110; Cimino, *Life at court*, no. 69. Although inscribed as depicting Raj Singh, this may be a portrait of his father Pratap Singh; cf. Pasricha, 'Painting at Sawar', figs. 3-4; Rajasthan Lalit Kala Akadami, *Varsika '63*, illus. p.1 (also S. Singh, *Catalogue*, no. 89, not illus.).

4. Lee, *Rajput painting*, no. 52; Patnaik, *A second paradise*, pl. 27. Cf. also Spink, *Krishnamandala*, fig. 68, for another bower crowded with perching birds. The bird theme again appears in a page from the large Sawar *Ramayana* (see no. 22), in which the crow recites scriptures to Garuda and the assembled pairs of birds (Kanoria coll., Patna: Arts Council, *In the image of man*, no. 393, not illus.).

5. Mathur, loc. cit. (reading *gān vidyā* for *gavan vidyā*, as kindly suggested by Dr Rupert Snell).

25
Maharaja Raj Singh of Junia at a jharokha window
Attributed to Chand
Junia, Rajasthan, c.1698
Brush drawing heightened with colour
52.2×46.3cm

It was the custom of the Mughal emperors from the time of Akbar until Aurangzeb to show themselves formally to the people each morning at a balcony window (*jharokha*) of their palaces. This formal window setting, with its textile-draped railing, became a common convention in both Mughal and Rajput portraiture[1] (see also no. 26). Here Maharaja Raj Singh of Junia, a small state in the Ajmer region, is depicted holding a rose, framed by a cusped window surround. He wears the tall turban of the Rathor clan,[2] a *jama* tied at his left shoulder, and jewellery, which like the rose and the ruler's lips has been lightly coloured. Although deriving from Mughal models by way of the mid-17th century Jodhpur school,[3] this portrait reveals the Rajput facility for abstraction in its resolution of form into bold outline drawing, complemented by light shading on the ruler's face and hands and the folds of cloth at his wrist. The cusped arch surround is only roughly sketched, as if an afterthought.

This painting belongs to a body of work attributable to the painter Chand, who worked for Raj Singh in the last years of the 17th century.[4] Like many of the more interesting Rajasthani artists, Chand was an eclectic with flair. His engaging style shows the influences of the major Rathor courts of Jodhpur and Bikaner, as well as that of Sawar (nos. 22-24), only twenty miles south of Junia. This study of Raj Singh is closely related to a larger, fully coloured painting in which Chand depicts his patron in similar pose and attire behind a low balustrade, holding a wine-cup instead of a flower and flanked by attendants, against a background of flowering trees[5] (fig. 3).

AT

Fig. 3 Raj Singh of Junia. Attributed to Chand, c.1700.
Kumar Sangram Singh of Nawalgarh collection, Jaipur.

1. For discussion see Weber, *Porträts,* pp.45-50.

2. Most of the Ajmer nobility were Rathors. In a l9th century British gazetteer they are described as "still war-like and indolent, and great consumers of opium" (*Rajputana Gazetteer,* II, Calcutta, 1879, p.36).

3. Cf. the portraits of Maharaja Gaj Singh (Khandalavala, Chandra and Chandra, *Miniature paintings,* col. pl. F; Desai, *Life at court,* no. 27) and Maharaja Jaswant Singh (Welch, *Indian drawings and painted sketches,* no. 64; Hodgkin and McInerney, *Indian drawing,* no. 49).

4. A portfolio of Chand's work was acquired some years ago by Kumar Sangram Singh of Nawalgarh (cf. S.Singh, *Catalogue,* pp.39-40). It bore a date equivalent to 1698 and the seal of Raj Singh, describing him as a *fidāwī* ("devoted servant") of the emperor Aurangzeb.

5. Collection of Kumar Sangram Singh, Jaipur. A further portrait of Raj Singh is in the Victoria & Albert Museum (I.S. 43-1979).

26
Maharaja Bakhat Singh of Nagaur

Nagaur or Jodhpur, Rajasthan, c.1730-35
Opaque watercolour on paper
43.5×30.5cm
A mutilated devanagari inscription on the reverse (the first line includes honorific titles, e.g. ...*śrī 108 śrī*; the second line reads: ...*vakhat siṅghjī*); also, various numerals (115, 73, 105), a rough sketch of a standing nobleman, and modern owners' inscriptions.

Maharaja Bakhat Singh (1706-53) appears at a *jharokha* window (see no. 25), holding a rose sprig in one hand. He has a flamboyant moustache and triangular sidewhiskers, and wears a turban with pink floral motifs on a green ground, a white *jama* with a bold iris pattern, as well as pearls and jewels. His dress and the architectural setting create a vibrant interplay of decorative floral pattern, offset by a pale green background. The finely detailed Mughal floral interlace of the carpet draped over the balcony (on which the Raja's diminutive, ringed fingers lightly rest) is balanced by the painted spandrels, which reflect the vogue for such mural decoration in the palaces of Marwar. The arch is similarly furnished with foliated scrolls of a type current at Jodhpur in the early 18th century,[1] and with pendant lotus forms which are also seen in Bikaner paintings of the same period.[2]

Bakhat Singh was the younger son of Maharaja Ajit Singh of Jodhpur. In 1724, when he was not yet 18, he murdered his father at the bidding of his brother Abhai Singh, who rewarded him with the territory of Nagaur. If this parricide was the crucial act of Bakhat Singh's life, he is otherwise remembered as a courageous and cultivated prince:

> There was a joyousness of soul about Bakhta which, united to an intrepidity and a liberality alike unbounded, made him the very model of a Rajput. To these qualifications were superadded a majestic mien and Herculean frame, with a mind well versed in all the literature of his country, besides poetic talent of no mean order...[3]

During the 1730s Bakhat Singh fought against Zorawar Singh of Bikaner and later with him against his own brother Abhai Singh. Eventually Bakhat Singh succeeded to the Jodhpur throne, but soon afterwards he was murdered, by means of a poisoned robe administered by a vengeful niece.[4]

Lying between the territories of Jodhpur, Bikaner and Ajmer, Nagaur was a constant object of dispute. It was once the furthest outpost of Muslim rule in Rajasthan, as well as being held by Bikaner or Jodhpur for long periods. Under Bakhat Singh's rule in the second quarter of the 18th century Nagaur flourished, and extant mural paintings in the palace apartments[5] date from this period. Nagaur painting of this time is often hardly distinguishable from Jodhpur work. Another closely related *jharokha* portrait of Bakhat Singh, inscribed with his name, is in the J. P. Goenka collection, Bombay[6] (fig. 4). The present painting and its companion piece in the National Gallery, Ottawa,[7] must count among the finest 18th century portraits from the Marwar region. They represent a superb fusion of the Mughal decorative aesthetic with the abstract simplicity of Rajput drawing.

Fig. 4 Maharaja Bakhat Singh of Nagaur and Jodhpur, c.1740.
J.P. Goenka collection, Bombay.

Published: Heeramaneck, *Masterpieces of Indian painting*, pl. 81.[8]

AT

1. Tillotson, *The Rajput palaces*, pp.139-40, fig. 167.

2. Cf. the portrait of a prince and lady in an enlarged jharokha setting, ascribed to Murad and dated 1729: Sotheby's New York sale cat., 2 Nov. 1988, lot 61; also Goetz, *Art and architecture of Bikaner*, fig. 81; Patnaik, *A second paradise*, pls. 28, 30 (Welch and Beach, *Gods, thrones and peacocks*, no. 30). A later 18th century picture of two ladies carousing (Archer, *Indian miniatures*, pl. 60, there attributed to Jaipur) has similar jharokha and rug patterns to the present painting.

3. Tod, *Annals*, II, p.1057.

4. Ibid., pp.866-67.

5. Goetz, 'Nagaur school', fig. 1: Goetz's description of a contemporary Nagaur style is unsound, as noted in *Kala Nidhi* (Benares), I, 2, p.90 fn.; see also Shukla, *Wall paintings of Rajasthan*, pp.14-20 and figs.

6. A further portrait of Bakhat Singh receiving a nobleman on a garden terrace (c.1740) is also in the Goenka collection. I am grateful to Robert Skelton and Rosemary Crill for bringing these pictures to my attention.

7. Heeramaneck, *Masterpieces of Indian painting*, pl. 82.

8. Also Parke-Bernet Galleries sale cat., New York, 21 Oct. 1965, lot 154; Sotheby's New York sale cat., 2 Nov. 1988, lot 63.

27

Maharaja Kirpal Pal of Basohli smoking

Mankot, Punjab Hills, c.1690
Opaque watercolour on paper
22.5×33cm

Raja Kirpal Pal sits cross-legged against a tasselled cushion on a patterned white floor-cloth spread over a striped durree. He holds the still smoking mouth-piece of his hookah lightly in two fingers, while his other hand rests on his bare heel. He wears a deep red *jama* and short *patka* (sash), cross-tied over a cummerbund, with a *katar* dagger tucked into it at the side. A jewelled pendant hangs at his chest. A *pan*-box and small spittoon stand before him. An attendant stands behind him with a fly-whisk and cloth, while a kneeling hookah-bearer inspects the *chilam* (pipe-bowl), in which he has deposited coals with his tongs.

This configuration of a seated raja smoking a hookah, with one or more attendants, became one of the most frequent conventions of portraiture in late 17th and early 18th century Hill painting. At the neighbouring courts of Basohli and Mankot in particular (see also no. 28), it allowed rich thematic variations of colour and pattern in backgrounds, costumes and carpets. Although shown taking his ease, the Raja remains a proud and imposing figure, with a hawkish eye. Little is known of Raja Kirpal Pal (r. c.1678-93), except that he was a devotee of Vishnu and Shiva, a successful warrior and a patron of learning and the arts, especially painting.[1] A number of comparable portraits of him are known.[2] This one is notable for its controlled intensity of colouring and delicate poise of composition. The respectful distance between Raja and servant is elegantly bridged by the undulating hookah tube.

AT

1. Archer, *Indian Paintings from the Punjab Hills*, I, p.17. Khandalavala, *N.C. Mehta collection*, p.13, suggests that Kirpal Pal lived until at least 1695.

2. Cf. Archer, op. cit., 'Mankot' no. 16 (also Randhawa, *Basohli painting*, pl. 1) and 'Basohli' no. 11(i) (also Davidson, *Los Angeles collections*, no. 129; Welch, *A flower from every meadow*, no. 35); Khandalavala, *Pahari miniature painting*, fig. 58; Randhawa, op. cit., pl. 3; Topsfield, 'Painting for the Rajput courts', fig. 185; Ehnbom, *Indian miniatures*, no. 86; Christie's sale cat., 11 June 1986, lot 23.

28
Maharaja Bhupat Pal of Basohli smoking
Mankot, c.1685
Opaque watercolour on paper
21×26.5cm

Seated on a boldly patterned carpet, Raja Bhupat Pal rests his arm against a cushion, while grasping the tube of a small, ornate hookah, supported by a kneeling servant holding coal-tongs. The prince wears a transparent white muslin *jama*, saffron-stained at the shoulders as for a ceremonial occasion, over a striped *paijama* (trousers), with a striped *patka* (sash) and a *katar* dagger and sword. Although this is ostensibly a scene of repose, the artist has set up an almost incongruously vivid interplay of colours and divergent textile patterns. Ruler and servant, of hierarchically differing size, are tautly linked by the diagonally slanting hookah tube. The composition is denser and more highly charged than that of *Maharaja Kirpal Pal smoking* (no. 27).

One of a number of portraits of Basohli rulers painted in the neighbouring and closely allied state of Mankot, this is a posthumous portrait of Bhupat Pal (r.1598-1635), the founder of Basohli town. He was imprisoned for fourteen years by the emperor Jahangir, but later became friendly with Shah Jahan. He was murdered at Delhi in 1635 by the scheming Raja of Nurpur. He is said to have been a man of very powerful physique, able to rub out the lettering on a rupee coin with his fingers. He daily consumed sixteen seers (nearly 15 kilos) of rice and one goat.[1]

A slightly earlier inscribed portrait of Bhupat Pal seated holding a sword was formerly in the Latifi collection, Bombay[2] (fig. 5), and others are in the Chandigarh Museum[3] and the National Museum, New Delhi.[4]

AT

Fig. 5 Raja Bhupat Pal of Basohli, c.1675.
Formerly Latifi collection, Bombay.

1. Archer, *Indian paintings from the Punjab Hills*, I, p.17.

2. Takri and Persian inscriptions both give the name Sri Raja Bhupat Pal Baluria. I am indebted to Dr Catherine Benkaim for this information.

3. Archer, op. cit., 'Mankot' no. 12; Goswamy, 'Essence and appearance', fig. 7.

4. See note 1.

29
Two ascetics making music
Illustration to the musical mode Kedara Raga
Arki (Baghal state), Punjab Hills, c.1700
Opaque watercolour on paper
21×18.5cm

A *sadhu* seated in half-lotus posture on a leopard skin plays the vina with rapt concentration, while his companion beats a rhythm with cymbals. They wear orange and yellow dhotis, with folds modelled in darker tones, and their ash-smeared skin is grey. They sit on a striped durree within a conventional pavilion setting, with a geometrically carved door half-open behind them at the centre of the composition. The yellow border and deep red background complement the more muted colouring of the pavilion interior.

From the 16th century onwards, *ragamala* ('Garland of Ragas') became one of the most popular subjects of Rajput painting. *Ragamala* illustrations were conceived as depicting the essential qualities of the North Indian musical modes, according to scenes prescribed by poetic texts. The principal ragas were grouped with their *raginis* or 'wives' in series of 36 or more paintings. In the Punjab Hills extended series of 84 pictures, including the 'sons' of ragas (*ragaputra*), were also current. This painting of Kedara, a *ragaputra* of Megha raga, belongs to one such series, which has been attributed to Arki, the capital of the small southerly Hill kingdom of Baghal, not far from Simla. Other pages from the series employ variations of the same pavilion setting.[1]

AT

1. Archer, *Indian paintings from the Punjab Hills*, 'Baghal (Arki)', nos. 2 (i-iii) [ibid., no. 2 (i) does not depict Kedara, as stated, but Kusuma, a *ragaputra* of Dipaka: cf. Waldschmidt and Waldschmidt, *Miniatures of musical inspiration*, I, pp.145-46; Ebeling, *Ragamala Painting*, p.288]; Archer, *Visions of courtly India*, nos. 2-3. See also Khandalavala, *Pahari miniature Painting*, supp. fig. 27; Pal, *The classical tradition*, no. 57; Tandan, *Pahari ragamalas*, p.96.

30
Harihara Sadashiva
Mandi, Punjab Hills, *c.*1710-20
Brush drawing, opaque watercolour on paper
33×27cm approx.

Sadashiva, the Eternal form of Shiva, whose five heads face the cardinal points and the zenith, is here shown in the form of Harihara, bearing the combined attributes of Shiva and Vishnu. In his five right hands he holds the trident, hand-drum, skullcup, sword and cobra of Shiva, and in his left hands, the mace, conch, discus and lotus of Vishnu as well as a shield. As the divine ascetic, Shiva sits cross-legged with long matted locks, wearing a leopard-skin, disc-shaped ear-rings and a necklace of human heads. He also wears certain items of princely jewellery, including thumb-rings used in archery. His eyes are turned upwards in yogic trance and his foreheads bear the third eye of insight. His heads and arms are festooned with garlands of the sacred datura plant.

This powerfully simplified image of the meditating god is related to a more fully coloured and detailed version of the same subject, in the Victoria and Albert Museum.[1] Both can be attributed to one of the most distinctive of Pahari (Hill) artists, the anonymous master who worked at Mandi in the first decades of the 18th century. His visualisation of Shiva was no doubt inspired by contemplation of the image of the god which is still in worship in the Panchavaktra temple at Mandi.[2] This version is perhaps even more starkly impressive than the V&A painting. The brush drawing is on a plain ground and only sparingly coloured, throwing into stronger relief the leopard skin pattern and the heavy stippled shading of the god's flesh.

The modelling of the massive hairy chest and belly recalls that of certain portraits of Raja Sidh Sen of Mandi (r.1684-1727),[3] for whom this picture was most probably painted. Sidh Sen is remembered as of a ruler of great physical stature and military prowess, who lived for nearly a hundred years. As a devotee of Shiva he had also acquired certain yogic powers. According to popular legend, he would magically fly to the source of the Ganges each morning to bathe, and family tradition has it that he would sometimes levitate while meditating before the image of Shiva in the palace.[4] Sidh Sen's self-identification with the god is reflected in a number of apotheosizing portraits, which show the ruler in ascetic guise or holding divine attributes in his multiple arms.[5]

AT

1. Archer, *Indian Paintings from the Punjab Hills*, I, p.356, 'Mandi' no. 15; Kramrisch, *Manifestations of Shiva*, no. P-9; Goswamy and Fischer, *Pahari-Meister*, no. 84; Crill, 'Rajput courts', pl. 126.

2. Archer, loc. cit. See also Goswamy and Fischer, op. cit., pp.190-93, for an essay on this Mandi master.

3. Archer, op. cit., 'Mandi' nos. 18 and 21 (also published in Desai, *Life at court*, no. 32, and Goswamy and Fischer, op. cit., no. 76; Khandalavala, *N.C. Mehta collection*, fig. 44).

4. Khandalavala, op. cit., p.109; Goswamy, *Essence*, no. 139.

5. Kramrisch, op. cit., no. P-16; Glynn, 'Seven inscribed Pahari portraits', figs. 1-4; Desai, op. cit., no. 81 (also Arts Council, *In the image of man*, no. 292, illus. p.48); Goswamy, op. cit., no. 138; idem, 'Essence and appearance', pp.198-99, fig. 5; Chandramani, 'On Mandi painting', figs. 483, 485.

31
An elephant eating from a tree
Mankot (?), Punjab Hills, early 18th century
Brush drawing, partially coloured
36.8×38.1cm

A royal elephant has been tethered near a tree, from which it is contentedly feeding. Having broken off a bough with its trunk, it holds it down with one foot while stripping away the leaves. The bearded mahout directs the meal with shouts of command and prods of the ankus (goad). The elephant is evidently enjoying a respite from state duties, as it wears processional trappings with bells, chains and a flowered saddle-cloth; the supporting pad for a howdah is also seen. A groom carrying a long goad with a pennant also sits on the elephant, while another contemplates the scene from the ground below.

In this unusual brush drawing the artist has captured a common scene of court life with freshness and wit, though his composition may derive in part from a Mughal source.[1] The textiles and costumes are sparsely coloured, and a pale wash has been applied to the elephant and the hastily outlined tree. Some details, such as the elephant's lumpish forefeet, show a lapse of observation. Elephants may for practical reasons have been less common at the Hill courts than in the plains of India.

Published: Hodgkin and McInerney, *Indian drawing*, no. 30.

AT

1. See no. 10, note 8, for a comparable Mughal study.

32
Angada delivers Rama's message to Ravana
Illustration to the 'Siege of Lanka' *Ramayana* series
Guler, Punjab Hills, c.1725
Opaque watercolour with gold on paper
60×82.5cm

This unfinished picture belongs to one of the largest and most famous series of Pahari paintings, known since its first publication by Coomaraswamy as the Siege of Lanka series.[1] Its subject, taken from the *Yuddhakanda* (Book 6) of the *Ramayana* epic (see also nos. 4, 22), is Rama's siege of the fortress of Lanka, where his wife Sita had been imprisoned by the demon king Ravana. Here Rama (with blue skin), his half-brother Lakshman, their new ally Vibhishana and the monkey and bear armies are camped on the mountain-side facing Ravana's golden palace. Rama's companions have reminded him of the need to enter into diplomacy with an enemy before committing oneself to battle. He has therefore sent the monkey prince Angada to tell Ravana that he must either yield Sita or be annihilated. Silhouetted in mid-air, Angada is seen crossing to the enemy fort with a flying leap; he then delivers his message to the many-headed Ravana in an audience-chamber, while leering demons stand around. Ravana of course does not heed Rama's ultimatum, and becomes enraged at Angada's denunciation of him. The next painting in the series shows Angada escaping from the palace with Ravana's crown.[2] After this the great battles would begin.

While the left half of the composition, including the figures of Angada, Ravana and the demons, is partly finished, Rama and his forces on the right are only in the preliminary stages of painting. The threateningly grouped armies of monkeys and bears appear as barely delineated grey and black masses. The fish and aquatic beasts in the foreground are similarly unfinished. This uneven distribution of surface detail accentuates the formal qualities of the dramatically simplified composition, comprising sky, ocean, hillside and golden fort, which recurs with variations in other pages from the series. This schematic setting was itself based on the landscape around the Guler rajas' fort at Haripur.

Probably commissioned by Raja Dalip Singh of Guler (r.1695-1741), the Siege of Lanka series may have comprised as many as a hundred pages. Forty are known to survive, mostly in museum collections in Boston and Bombay. When work on the series was discontinued, only nine pages had been finished, four (as here) were left partly finished, and the rest remained as uncoloured drawings. Although it has been suggested that such large pictures were intended as cartoons for wall-paintings, the fine quality of the completed pages indicates that they were intended as finished works in their own right, probably for display at *Ramayana* recitations or story-telling sessions in the palace at Guler.

Published: Jain-Neubauer, *The Ramayana*, p.42, figs. 31-33; McInerney, *Indian painting*, no. 34; Craven, *Ramayana: Pahari paintings*, no. 10, pp.40-41.

AT

1. Coomaraswamy, *Raiput painting*, pp.59-60; idem, *Catalogue...Museum of Fine Arts, Boston*, V, pp.78-84. For discussions of the series, see Archer, *Indian paintings from the Punjab Hills*, I, pp.146-47; Jain-Neubauer, *The Ramayana*, pp.14-21, 37-49; Welch, *India*, no. 272; Leach, *Indian miniature paintings*, no. 113; and, most recently, Goswamy and Fischer, *Pahari-Meister*, no. 99 and pp.243ff (with an attribution to the painter Manaku, son of Pandit Seu); and Craven, *Ramayana: Pahari paintings*, pp.2-66, with many illustrations.

2. Metropolitan Museum, New York: Jain-Neubauer, op. cit., fig. 34; Craven, op. cit., pl. 11, pp.42-43: this page is in a more unfinished state than the present one.

33
A fly-infested feast
Chamba (?), Punjab Hills, mid-18th century
Brush drawing, partially coloured, on paper
41×59cm

This strange scene of priests and courtiers feasting in a fly-infested enclosure is an example of the comic undercurrent occasionally found in Rajput painting. An unidentified prince and his entourage attend a meal with an assembly of Brahmins in an open air refectory. In the shade of a grass-roofed shelter, the head priest and his younger deputy, in pink dhotis, and the prince, in white *jama* and turban, eat off silver trays (the rest of the company have leaf plates). Vigorous swatting with cloths by the three priestly attendants has partly cleared the air around them of the flies which elsewhere envelop the proceedings. These red-headed insects swarm thickest near the waiters, feasters and cooks under their shelter.[1] Even so, the two portly Brahmins seated at the far right still munch their rice impassively, as do their junior colleagues in the foreground and the nobles and younger male relatives of the prince to the left. Only one or two of the standing waiters have a slightly depressed air. A stern-looking group of the prince's attendants and courtiers observes the scene from beyond the rustic fence. The artist's pentimenti appear here, and elsewhere in the picture.

The meaning of this unusual subject remains unclear. Some satire may well be intended on the complacent venality of the priestly class,[2] and perhaps on the princeling who is ingratiating himself with them. A large drawing of an elaborate shrine, also in the Hodgkin collection, is in a related style.[3]

Published: Welch, *Indian drawings*, no. 75; Hodgkin and McInerney, *Indian drawing*, no. 44.

AT

1. Compare a Kulu artist's bee swarm in Pal, *The classical tradition*, no. 70.

2. Cf. Goswamy, *Essence*, no. 78.

3. Hodgkin and McInerney, *Indian drawing*, no. 41.

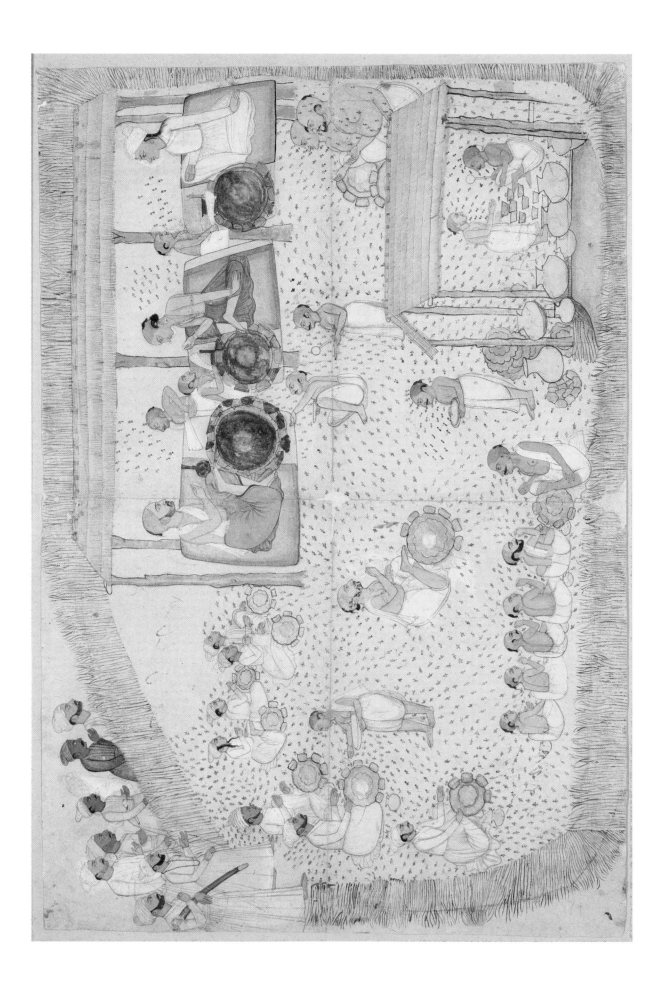

34
The disrobing of Draupadi
Attributed to Nainsukh (?)
Guler style at Basohli, Punjab Hills, c.1765
Opaque watercolour with gold on paper
24.6×34.2cm
Inscribed in takri and devanagari scripts with the characters' names.

In a famous episode from the second book of the *Mahabharata* epic, the five Pandava brothers and their joint wife Draupadi are dispossessed and humiliated by their cousins and rivals, the Kauravas. The virtuous Yudhishthira, eldest of the Pandavas, has rashly gambled away their wealth, their liberty and even their wife in the disastrous dice game which will lead to their exile. Duhshasana, one of the Kaurava princes, drags Draupadi into the audience hall and attempts to denude her. But her honour is miraculously preserved:

> Then Duhshasana forcibly laid hold of Draupadi's robe, and in the midst of the assembly began to undress her. But when her skirt was being stripped off, another similar skirt appeared every time. A terrible roar went up from all the kings, a shout of approval, as they watched that greatest wonder on earth…
> A pile of clothes was heaped up in the middle of the hall, when Duhshasana, tired and ashamed, at last desisted and sat down.[1]

Duhshasana is shown tugging veil after veil from Draupadi's head. She stands amid the growing heap of clothing stripped from her. The Pandava brothers sit nearby in a dejected group. Yudhishthira, a finger held to his lip in bewilderment, lays a restraining hand on the knee of the volatile, mace-bearing Bhima. Nakula and Sahadeva commiserate, while Arjuna sits slumped forward. These foreground figures are set against a long durree, boldly striped in brown on red. Its superimposed pattern partly obscures the abandoned cloth *chaupar* board on which the fatal dice game has been played (the three oblong ivory dice, however, are painted over the carpet colours). Above, the blind king Dhritarashtra presides over the durbar, while his eldest son, Duryodhana, leader of the Kauravas, gesticulates towards Draupadi. He will offer further insult by showing her his bared thigh. Other Kaurava princes sit on either side (one of them half-obscured by a pillar), together with two standing attendants.

More expansive Guler versions of this subject, with a greater number of figures, are in the Lahore[2] and Chandigarh[3] Museums, and a further related version is in the Victoria and Albert Museum.[4] Compared with these, the present scene is composed with particular economy and finesse. Draupadi standing among her swirling, multi-coloured veils[5] is also a less demurely acquiescent figure; her pose conveys her scornful resistance to Duhshasana's assault. This rendering of the subject could well be a late work by Nainsukh, one of the most distinguished of all Pahari artists, or else the work of a close follower. A son of the influential painter Pandit Seu of Guler, Nainsukh is celebrated for his highly original portrait work for his patron Raja Balwant Singh of Jasrota or Jammu. After Balwant Singh's death in 1763, he entered the service of Raja Amrit Pal of Basohli, for whom he appears to have worked on illustrations to poetical or mythological series.[6] The facial types, the poised figure drawing, the tripartite division of the durbar hall[7] and details such as the furled blinds with hanging ties are all redolent of Nainsukh's style. The striking red and brown carpet is also a Guler convention[8] of which he made use.[9]

AT

1. van Buitenen tr., *Mahabharata*, II, p.146.

2. Aijazuddin, *Pahari paintings*, Guler no. 30.

3. Coomaraswamy, *Rajput painting*, pl. XXXVIIa.

4. Ibid., pl. XXXVI; Archer, *Indian paintings from the Punjab Hills*, Guler no. 14. See also ibid., Jammu no. 70, for a later related painting of the dice game in progress.

5. For a later version, cf. Goswamy, *Essence*, no. 196.

6. For a recent account of Nainsukh's career, see Goswamy and Fischer, *Pahari-Meister*, pp.268-77 and nos. 112-29; also Archer, op. cit., s.v. Jammu, *passim*.

7. Cf. Aijazuddin, op. cit., Jammu no. 2, col. pl. XII; Goswamy and Fischer, op. cit., no. 125.

8. Khandalavala, *Pahari miniature paintings in the N.C. Mehta collection*, col. pl. F; Archer, op. cit., Guler no. 33 and commentary.

9. Ibid., Jammu no. 34; Goswamy and Fischer, op. cit., no. 128.

35
Rao Madho Singh of Kota hunting wild boar
Kota, Rajasthan, c.1740
Opaque and transparent watercolour on paper
50×62.2cm

The seemingly rapid execution of the brushwork and the free, loose application of pigment suggests that this is an unusually spontaneous work, one in which the style perfectly matches the rapidity and control necessary to the action it depicts. Recent research has shown, however, that it is actually a close copy of an earlier wall-painting in the palace at Bundi, and a composition that was probably frequently repeated in the interim.[1] This is not unusual. Wall-paintings and works on paper are often closely related in theme and style. More important, however, is the ensuing realization that – for Indian artists – neither artistic quality nor spontaneity of execution were dependent on compositional originality (see also no. 14).

Kota was not acknowledged as an independent territory until 1631; its lands, until then, were part of Bundi State. Madho Singh (r.1631-48), the first ruler of Kota, was the second son of Rao Ratan Singh of Bundi (r.1607-31). Many of the artists who moved to Kota therefore took with them artistic standards already established at the older court. Since Madho Singh was the founder of Kota State, posthumous portraits of him were especially common.

MCB

1. See Bautze, 'Portraits of Rao Ratan and Madho Singh Hara', especially figs. 12 and 14 – the latter being a later version of the same composition. Dr Bautze dates the Badal Mahal painting to c.1630, but it is the later work which bears an inscribed identification of Madho Singh. For another work by the artist of the version under discussion, see Welch, *India*, no. 245.

36

An elephant hunt
Kota, Rajasthan, c.1745
Opaque watercolour and gold on paper
46.3×52.1cm

As female wild elephants and their young sport in a lotus pond, an enraged male rushes at two intruding elephants, whose riders – partly camouflaged by leaves in their turbans and belts – are intent on capturing part of the herd. At the top, the male has been harnessed; with a trained elephant on either side, he is led away. Horsemen in front shoot arrows to help control the beast, while a man sits in a tree with ropes ready to add to the captive's fetters as he passes beneath[1]. Such continuous narratives – in which several sequential episodes of an event are seen in one image – are typical of Rajput painting (see also nos. 19-21, 32, 39, 42). Mughal painting in its heyday instead most often isolated individual moments into separate illustrations (see nos. 1 and 3).

Because it is a continuous narrative, the composition is more densely packed than *Rao Madho Singh of Kota hunting wild boar* (no. 35), but the vegetation types and the brushwork are nonetheless similar. Again a Mughal prototype exists (fig. 6),[2] but while it is thematically similar, the viewer is aware there that a vast scene is being presented in small scale – it follows the aesthetic of miniature paintings. Here, on the other hand, the artist creates such energy that the scene is barely contained within its borders.

Published: Welch, *A flower from every meadow*, no. 22; Colnaghi and Co., *Indian painting*, no. 70.

MCB

Fig. 6 Elephants bathing.
Mughal, c.1640.
Islamisches Museum, Staatliche Museen,
Berlin (F.4596, fol. 16).

1. A closely related painting in the Chester Beatty Library, Dublin, shows the process of attaching ropes to the wild elephant under a tree: see Topsfield, 'Painting for the Rajput courts', fig. 179. For a comparable subject from Bikaner, cf. Smart and Walker, *Pride of the princes*, no. 40.

2. See also Hickmann and Enderlein, *Indische Albumblätter*, pl. 23 and p. 147.

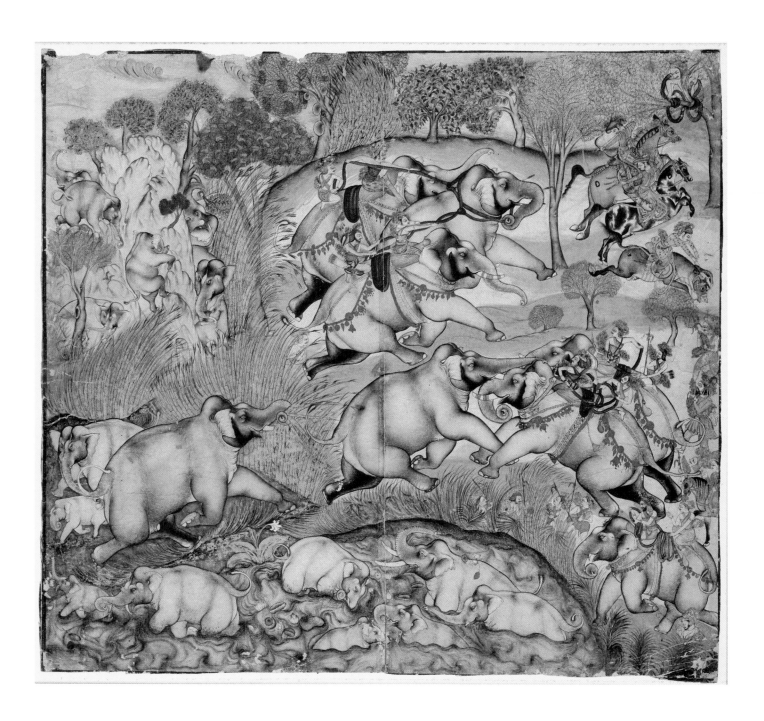

37

Maharao Durjan Sal and Shri Brijnathji hunting tigers and wild buffalo

Kota, Rajasthan, second quarter of the 18th century
Opaque watercolour with gold on cotton cloth
102.4×191.3cm

At the upper right, Maharao Durjan Sal of Kota (r.1723-56), is depicted on elephant-back, chasing a wild buffalo. Men watch this activity from the safety of nearby trees or hilltops as drummers and beaters drive the game towards the hunting party – it is clearly a lively and noisy occasion.

The event could never actually have taken place, however, for facing Durjan Sal is the blue-skinned Shri Brijnathji, a manifestation of the god Krishna. Brijnathji has been considered the supreme deity of the Kota family since 1719, when Maharao Bhim Singh I (r.1707-20) became so devoted to the god that he proclaimed himself merely the Diwan (Prime Minister) of Brijnathji. The temple he established in the Kota palace is still active today.[1] Numerous depictions of Shri Brijnathji show him being attended or worshipped by Kota rulers, or even leading the life of a Kota prince – such imagery of Krishna had long been accepted.[2] Several scenes of Brijnath hunting are known, and they seem to have become especially popular during the reign of Durjan Sal.[3] Here the god is shown as if he were leading the Kota royal family, an appropriately symbolic placement. Several of the figures are identified by inscription, and while many of these inscriptions are unclear or partially obliterated, the following names can be read: Maharao Durjan Sal, son of Bhim Singh (upper right); [Ra]m Singh (r.1695-1707), son of Kishor Singh (r.1684-95) and also Durjan Sal's grandfather (centre left); and Madho Singh Jhala, the brother-in-law of Durjan Sal (centre right).[4]

Wall-paintings in the Chattar Mahal section of Kota Palace, while later in date and even then heavily repainted, are very similar to this scene.[5] This work has itself been slightly restored. It was almost certainly made to hang in a tent complex, as an equivalent for the mural decoration necessary to palace architecture.

MCB

1. Brijraj Singh, *The kingdom that was Kotah*, p.14.

2. For a scene showing Brijnath being worshipped by Maharao Arjun Singh (r.1720-23), see Brijraj Singh, op. cit., pl. V. An image of Brijnathji being worshipped within the Kota temple is reproduced in Desai, *Life at court*, no. 98. See also Bautze, 'Zur Darstellung der Hauptgottheiten Kotas'.

3. See especially Brijraj Singh, op. cit., pl. III. A preparatory drawing for this scene, in a private collection, identifies the royal hunter there as Rao Bhoj, a common ancestor of the Bundi and Kota rulers, who is frequently mentioned in such scenes. That the same scene is identified by inscriptions with two different rulers indicates that inscriptions are as often acts of homage as historical documentation. For a scene of Brijnath hunting at night, dated 1781, see Beach, *Rajput painting at Bundi and Kota*, fig. 92.

4. Maharao Arjun Singh had married the sister of Madhu Singh Jhala, but died childless. He was succeeded by his younger brother Durjan Sal.

5. Beach, *Rajput painting at Bundi and Kota*, figs. 114-15; and Brijraj Singh, *The wonder that was Kotah*, figs. 47-48.

38
A lady singing

Kishangarh, Rajasthan, c.1740
Opaque and transparent watercolour with gold on paper
37×25.5cm
Inscribed on the back in devanagari script: *sabī nāyakā gātī huī* ("Picture of a *nāyikā* [an ideal heroine] singing"); numbered (40); modern stamp of the Officer of the Wardrobe (*kapad bhandar āfisar*), Kishangarh State.

Her lips slightly parted in song, the lady plucks a green and gilt tanpura, which divides the page diagonally. With her other, somewhat disembodied hand she shows a hennaed palm in an expressive gesture. Her long tresses and her shoulders are overlaid by a transparent *dupatta*, rendered in broad washes and bold strokes of thin colour. This unusually free brushwork is sometimes found in painting at Kishangarh, a small state close to Ajmer, around the mid-18th century. More typical of Kishangarh are the lady's features, with their pronounced profile, arching eyebrow and elongated, lotus-like eye.

This distinctive ideal of physical beauty developed under the patronage of Maharaja Raj Singh (r.1706-48), who employed several painters from Delhi, and of his son Savant Singh (r.1748-64). Both rulers were followers of the Vallabhacarya sect of Krishna worship, and Savant Singh was himself a well-known devotional poet under the name Nagari Das. The sober Mughal conventions originally practised by their artists evolved into a lyrical and ultimately mannered expression of Vaishnava poetic feeling, in which the divine consorts Krishna and Radha were depicted together in idyllic landscape and palace settings. According to legend, these scenes reflect Savant Singh's inseparability from the singer and poetess Bani Thani, who later accompanied him when he gave up the throne in 1757 to retire to the holy town of Vrindavan.[1]

The lady in the picture is described in the inscription as a *nayika*, or an ideal heroine as classified in poetic tradition. She seems to represent an idealised study, on an enlarged scale, of the type of female court musician seen elsewhere as minor figures at royal concert parties.[2] This study is related to other freely rendered brush drawings of female subjects, in Los Angeles[3] and San Francisco[4] museum collections. Deriving from a Mughal portrait convention, they too are more embodiments of an ideal of feminine beauty than studies of individuals.[5] In this fine example, while the Kishangarh facial type is in evidence, it does not yet approach the full-blown mannerism of a half-figure painting of Radha in the Kishangarh Palace collection.[6]

AT

1. Dickinson and Khandalavala, *Kishangarh painting*, pp.8-12.

2. Ibid., pl. X: e.g. the figure in the centre foreground, identified by the authors as Pokhraj, a singer from Shahjahanabad (Delhi).

3. Pal et al., *Romance of the Taj Mahal*, pl. 8.

4. Ehnbom, *Indian miniatures*, no. 72 (also McInerney, *Indian painting*, no. 27; *Archives of Asian Art*, XLII, 1989, p.104); now in the Asian Art Museum of San Francisco.

5. Kishangarh singing-girls were not always depicted so decorously. Just as the mature Kishangarh style relied for its effect on certain extraordinary distortions of physical form, so there also co-existed with its idealised poetic vision an earthy undercurrent of satire, in which these ladies among others could sometimes be shown in grotesquely unpoetic ways: e.g. Welch, *Indian drawings*, no. 66; idem, *India: Art and culture*, no. 250 (also Patnaik, *Second paradise*, pl. 34).

6. Dickinson and Khandalavala, op. cit., pl. IV. Cf. also Kramrisch, *Painted delight*, no. 75, and Welch and Beach, *Gods, thrones and peacocks*, no. 55 (and cover illus.).

39

Maharana Jagat Singh II of Mewar with his queens at Jagniwas palace

By Sukha and Syaji
Udaipur, Rajasthan, 1751
Opaque watercolour with gold and silver on paper
112.8×57.6cm

Inscribed on the back in devanagari script (fig. 7): *śrī rāmjī 1/śrī māhārājadhīrāja māhārāṇājī śrī jagat sīghjī rī surat rā pano jaganīvās rā bhāv rā kātī vadī 7 some smat 1808 baraṣai kalamī cītāro sukho syajī*. (Shri Ramji. Picture of the likeness of Maharajadhiraja Maharana Jagat Singh at Jagniwas; Monday the 7th of the dark half of Karttik, in the year V.S. 1808; by the painters Sukha and Syaji).

Maharana Jagat Singh II (r.1734-51) was a hedonistic and ineffectual ruler, in whose reign the proudly independent kingdom of Mewar was forced to pay tribute to the expansionist Marathas from the south. His career was thus assessed by Tod, the first British Political Agent at Udaipur (1818-22):

> Addicted to pleasure, his habits of levity and profusion totally unfitted him for the task of governing his country at such a juncture; he considered his elephant fights of more importance than keeping down the Mahrattas. Like all his family, he patronized the arts, greatly enlarged the palace, and expended £250,000 in embellishing the islets of the Pichola...Many of those festivals devoted to idleness and dissipation, and now firmly rooted at Udaipur, were instituted by Jagat Singh II.[1]

This elaborate painting, still impressive in spite of damage and fading of the pigments, celebrates what was probably Jagat Singh's favourite architectural achievement, the island palace of Jagniwas, where amid the breezes of the Pichola lake he would disport with his companions in the sultry summer months. This project is said to have been inspired by the earlier unwillingness of his father Sangram Singh II to allow him to occupy the existing lake palace of Jagmandir with his zenana ladies.[3] Jagniwas was founded in March 1743, the year in which Jagat Singh had for a time ceased to pay the Maratha tribute,[4] and it was inaugurated with lavish ceremony on 1 February 1746.[5] It remained largely unaltered until the early 1960s, when it was remodelled as the Lake Palace Hotel.

Five consecutive scenes are shown, from the events of a day spent by Jagat Singh mainly in the company of his fourteen queens and their attendants. In the far distance, the Maharana has arrived by barge at the Vaidyanath Mahadeva temple on the western shore of the Pichola lake. This temple had been built by Jagat Singh's grandmother, and early in 1716, at the age of six, he had accompanied the royal women to its inauguration ceremony.[6] After processing up an avenue of *qanat* purdah screens, he and his queens are shown worshipping the Shiva *lingam*.

Arriving at the lake palace below, Jagat Singh is welcomed by his queens, standing in the further of two carpeted courtyards. Four women escort him, one of them holding up his trailing *jama* skirts. On the roof terrace to the left, the same company are seated for refreshments. They are also throwing some substance at one another, perhaps a perfume, while a dancer and musicians perform. In the carpeted central courtyard below, Jagat Singh and his ladies sit watching as six dancers enact the Rasmandala or round dance of Krishna and the cow-girls, to a musical accompaniment. This scene accords with Jagat Singh's known taste for the *Raslila* dance dramas.[7]

During these purdah revels, Jagat Singh's male courtiers have been segregated in the garden courtyard in the foreground. They are shown standing formally in attendance or gossiping in the corner *chhatris*, while their chief practises archery on the fish in the lake.[8] The arcade at the rear of this courtyard is notable for the

Fig. 7 Inscription on reverse of no. 39.

imaginative interpretation of the Dutch or Chinese tiles which formerly adorned it. While the horizontal band of tiles portrays the Hindu gods and their exploits, the vertical bands mainly depict erotic scenes of various kinds, including several *firangi* (European) couples.[9]

The artists Syaji and Sukha had collaborated on another large work for Jagat Singh in the previous year (1750).[10] The present composition, unusually, has been elongated vertically to include the temple scene on the far shore of the lake. It is a striking example of what was almost a sub-genre of lake palace views in mid-18th century Udaipur painting.[11] It is also a revealing record of the private hours of this escapist Rana. As in the case of his grandfather Amar Singh in his rose-garden (no. 20), all of this was vanity. When this picture was entered into the royal store in late October 1751, Jagat Singh had already died in June, at the age of 41. Some at least of his fourteen queens would also then have perished in the flames of suttee.

AT

1. Tod, *Annals and antiquities*, I, p.495.

2. The painting has at some time been trimmed at the edges and displayed in a frame, thus exposing it to excessive light. The yellows and greens have faded most, leaving the hills and vegetation with a pronounced pink tinge. Traces of the original yellow-green pigments survive at the edges where they were concealed by the picture frame. A trace of the original red border also remains at the top edge.

3. Shyamaldas, *Vir vinod*, II, p.1233.

4. Gupta, *Mewar and the Maratha relations*, p.57.

5. The poet Nand Ram described the occasion in some detail in his *Jagat Vilas:* Shyamaldas, op. cit., pp.1234-35.

6. A contemporary painting of this event is in the Shiv Niwas Palace collection at Udaipur. Its inscription is quoted in full by Shyamaldas, op. cit., pp.956-57. The Vaidyanath temple is likely to have remained a favourite place of worship for the royal ladies thereafter, and also for Jagat Singh. For a painting in a more mythological idiom probably showing him (not his father Sangram Singh, as inscribed) having darshan of Shiva at the same temple, see Topsfield, *Paintings from Rajasthan*, no. 87.

7. For the series of paintings depicting the *Raslila* plays performed for Jagat Singh in 1736, see Topsfield, 'Udaipur paintings of the Raslila'.

8. A related painting by Jai Ram, entered into the royal picture store by the same clerk on the same day in 1751, shows Jagat Singh bathing with his ladies in a pool on Jagniwas and again shooting the fish from this balcony (Mewar royal collection, unpublished). The motif appears

again in Ari Singh's reign: cf. Goswamy, *Essence*, no. 74, which is a reworking of the present composition, again showing the figurative tilework *in situ*; see also Topsfield, *The City Palace Museum*, no. 22.

9. Such exotic tiles were first used in the Chini ki Chitrasali of the City Palace during the reign of Maharana Sangram Singh, and were later incorporated by Jagat Singh in the Pitam Niwas apartments (Shyamaldas, op. cit, p.1245; see also Topsfield, 'Ketelaar's embassy', notes 47, 51). They were later several times reinterpreted in paintings with fanciful or erotic imagery, e.g. in Bakhta's view of the Pitam Niwas dated 1765: Topsfield, *Paintings from Rajasthan*, no. 167, col. pl. 14.

10. Topsfield, *The City Palace Museum*, no. 11; also ibid., no 16.

11. This began in Sangram Singh II's reign after his additions to Jagmandir, notably with the crocodile feeding scene of c.1720 at Melbourne (Topsfield, *Paintings from Rajasthan*, no. 72; Desai, *Life at court*, no. 53, with implausible dating); see also Khandalavala and Doshi, *A collector's dream*, illus. pp.100-1. It continued with scenes of Jagat Singh's sports on Jagmandir (Welch, *A flower*, no. 8; Kramrisch, *Painted delight*, no. 68), and later on Jagniwas: cf. n.8 above, and Cimino et al., *Life at court*, no. 71 and col. pl. (also Tillotson, *The Rajput palaces*, col. pl. XII). Welch and Beach, *Gods thrones and peacocks*, no. 34 (also Welch, *India*, no. 254) appears to be a study of Jagniwas prior to or at an early stage of its development by Jagat Singh. This sub-genre culminated with the great Jagmandir picture of Maharana Ari Singh dated 1767: Topsfield, *The City Palace Museum*, no. 22.

40

Rawat Gokul Das of Deogarh shooting fowl by a lake

By Bakhta

Deogarh (Mewar), Rajasthan, 1806

Opaque watercolour with gold and silver on paper

54×79cm

Inscribed on the back in devanagari script (fig. 8): *mhāravatjī śrī 5 śrī gokal dāsjī kī surat: talāv sīg sāgar kau bhāv mhail sund/ muḍhā āgai kākaujī rāvat ?gyan sighjī/ tīrai bhādau amarjī* [*sam*] *1863 rā: dutī sāvaṇ* [*bad*] *12 saumai din pānau najar vhau darīkhānai barājya* [*del.: kalamī ca*]/*kalamī catāro bakhatau:*. ("The likeness of Maharavat Shri Gokul Das at the Sig (Singh?) Sagar [Lion Lake], accompanied by the uncle Ravat Gyan(?) Singh and Amarji; presented in the (?) pavilion on Monday 12th of the dark half of Sravan V.S.1863. By the painter Bakhta.") Below this, an indistinct inscription brushed in red paint, together with a sketch of a face, also gives the artist's name, Bagta (*sic*).

As a result of political and economic disruption, painting at Udaipur (nos. 19-21, 39) went into temporary decline from the late 1760s. The court artists either gave up their trade or found patronage with the leading Mewar nobles. At Deogarh, 80 miles to the north-east, a vigorous variant of the Udaipur style was to flourish for the next three generations. Its senior and most gifted exponent was Bakhta (or Bagta), who had begun his career at Udaipur in the 1750s.[1] Bakhta's ability seems only to have increased with maturity. Several of his finest pictures were painted in his old age, especially during his late flowering of c.1806-08, the period to which the present painting belongs. It celebrates, in abundant detail, the various sports of Rawat Gokul Das (r.1786-1821) in and around the Singh Sagar (Lion Lake) near Deogarh. Gokul Das was remembered by Tod as a commanding figure, "...one of the finest men I ever beheld in feature and person. He was about six feet six, perfectly erect, and a Hercules in bulk."[2] However, he was a greedily rapacious ruler. His long-suffering subjects complained to Tod, among many other matters, that "if any one have a good horse, by fair means or foul he contrives to get it".[3]

This picture in some ways recalls the genre of lake palace views established earlier at Udaipur (no. 39). But unlike many Udaipur compositions, in which the action is carefully structured around an architectural or landscape setting, Bakhta has not composed a coherent panoramic view so much as a dense and brilliant assemblage of minutely observed scenes and bravura passages. Gokul Das himself appears on a rocky promontory in the foreground, where he shoots waterfowl in the company of his uncle Rawat Gyan(?) Singh and another courtier named Amarji. He again appears three times within the combined shooting-box and pleasure pavilion set on a small island in the lake. There he consorts with his zenana ladies, performs his toilet and does some more shooting from a corner turret. On the shore to the left, the Rawat's numerous escort, together with his elephant, horses, camels and the bullock-drawn purdah carriages, take their ease beneath the trees, while the cooks prepare a meal. Grooms wash horses in the shallows, while dhobis (washermen) and fishermen are at work around the lake, and villagers labour in the fields.

The often tiny scale of such scenes does not lend itself to a cursory viewing. The same is true of the extraordinarily vital treatment of the landscape and wildlife. The rocks in the foreground are fluidly outlined and shaded in molten, animated shapes. Among them, above a bund wall, is a luxuriant grove of flowering trees and plantains, with numerous birds, peacocks and darting, agile monkeys. Other notable passages include the further wooded islet in the lake, with its waterfowl and benignly basking or prancing crocodiles.

The work is a joyous celebration of the Deogarh landscape and of the ruler's pleasure in it. As such, it forms a contrast with Bakhta's other great painting of 1806, the durbar scene of Gokul Das, completed a few months later,[4] in the National Museum, New Delhi. There he is more concerned with the human peculiarities – verging on caricature – of the assembled courtiers, while the landscape is little more than a strongly coloured backdrop. These two pictures, together with the hunt picnic of 1808 in Bombay,[5] are among the most remarkable works of Bakhta's maturity.

AT

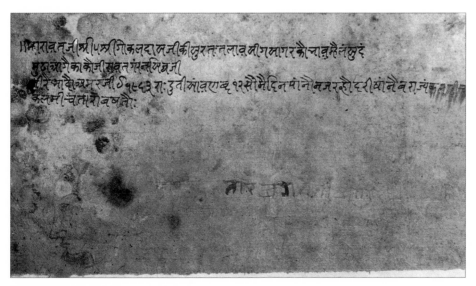

Fig. 8 Inscription on reverse of no. 40.

1. Topsfield, *Paintings from Rajasthan*, nos. 130, 167; Cimino et al., *Life at court*, no. 40; also Topsfield, *The City Palace Museum*, no. 23. Bakhta's earliest dated work is a conventional equestrian portait of Maharana Raj Singh II dated 1756 (present location unknown), in which he is described as the son of Pema. Bakhta's earliest known work at Deogarh is the dynamic hunting portrait of Prince Anup Singh of 1769: Andhare and Singh, *Deogarh painting*, pl. II.

2. Tod, *Annals and antiquities*, I, p.221n.

3. Ibid., pp.230-32.

4. Beach, 'Painting at Devgarh', figs. 9-10. The inscription gives the date of presentation of the painting as V.S. 1863 *pos sud* 10 (December 1806/January 1807): I am grateful to Milo Beach for providing a photograph.

5. Andhare, 'Painting from the thikana of Deogarh', pp.46-47 and frontispiece; Beach, op. cit., fig. 13; Andhare and Singh, op. cit., pl. I; Gorakhshkar et al., *Skönhetens Spegel*, no. 121.

Cat. no. 40 *(detail)*

41
A court beauty

Attributed to Chokha
Udaipur, Rajasthan, c.1810-20
Opaque watercolour with gold and silver on cotton cloth
123×61cm
Inscribed above: *phutaḍya* ("A beauty"), with a valuation (10 rupees) on the right spandrel of the white arch. Another, fainter valuation (15 rupees) appears on the blue background to the left of the lady's arms.

Within the frame of a Mewari cusped arch, a nubile beauty stretches her joined hands overhead in an attitude of love-longing. Her huge lotus-petal eye is dreamily abstracted. The ends of her dark hair are electrically wild. Her swollen breasts, scarcely constrained by the transparent *choli*, support long swinging strings of pearls. Her hip is out-thrust at a complementary angle to her jutting bosom. Her flaring skirts, orange and crimson with tie-dyed lozenges, contrast vividly with the blue background. Identified simply as "a beauty", she is an idealised figure of a size and type often found in Rajput palace wall-paintings. It is also conceivable that she might represent a favourite queen or concubine of the hedonistic Maharana Bhim Singh of Mewar (r.1778-1828). Beside her, a chubby, bejewelled infant – perhaps one of Bhim Singh's hundred or more children – bids for her attention, also with arms outstretched. The crescent moon, emblem of Shiva, at his forehead distinguishes his royal Sisodia birth.

This arresting interpretation of a conventional feminine pose[1] is all the more powerful for its large size and assured execution.[2] Its treatment of the female form even recalls earlier Indian sculptural traditions, as seen for example in an 11th century figure of a playful maiden from Nagda in Mewar.[3] The present lady's voluptuous abandon is quite unlike the wooden female studies by other contemporary Mewar painters, and also recalls the similar attitude and *tribhanga* (triple-flexed) pose of a late 17th century Golconda beauty.[4]

This picture may be attributed to Chokha (fl. c.1799-1824), son of Bakhta (no. 40), who worked both at Deogarh and the royal capital of Udaipur at different times. He evolved an expressive and idiosyncratic style, in which squat, well-fleshed, stipple-shaded figures often appear absorbed in sensuous reverie. Chokha's sources were eclectic but he treated them with verve. The lady's profile and elongated eye derive from earlier Kishangarh models (no. 38). The beseeching child is an unusual figure, since infants are generally scarce in Rajasthani painting, and it may derive ultimately from a European source. An anologous figure appears in an early 19th century exoticist painting, possibly by Chokha, in which a small European princeling seeks the attention of a Chinese lady.[5] Again within Chokha's own family tradition, a comparable grouping of a lady with upraised arms and a child to her left occurs among the surviving wall-paintings at the Deogarh palace.[6] The present work could itself perhaps duplicate a palace mural which is now lost. A comparable cloth-painting attributable to Chokha, of slightly smaller dimensions but with the same blue background and careful modelling of its subject's hairy flesh, is the portrait of Maharana Bhim Singh with a hawk, in the Ashmolean Museum, Oxford.[7]

AT

1. The gesture of hands clasped overhead, expressing luxuriant ease or love-longing, is found (in a seated figure) in the iconography of Desavarati *ragini*, e.g. Dahmen-Dallapiccola, *Ragamala-Miniaturen*, pp.281ff.; see also Waldschmidt, *Miniatures of musical inspiration*, II, pp.141ff. For examples of similar standing figures, cf. e.g. Zebrowski, *Deccani painting*, pl. 233; Maggs Bros. Bulletin, 16, London, 1970, no. 7b.

2. A small and more restrained version of this subject, painted on paper with the white background often used by Chokha in his late period (c.1820-24), was shown at the Tooth Gallery, London, in 1978. A still later version, by a follower of Chokha, is in the Patna Museum: Goswamy, *Essence*, no. 36.

3. Arts Council, *In the image of man*, no. 69 and p.57 (col. pl.); Goswamy, op. cit., no. 4.

4. Welch, *A flower from every meadow*, no. 81; Zebrowski, op. cit., pl. 177; Patnaik, *The second paradise*, pl. 10.

5. Topsfield, 'Ketelaar's embassy', fig. 20. Compare also a Europeanised subject of a mother and suckling infant (with crescent moon at its forehead) in Chokha's style: Doris Wiener Gallery sale cat., New York, 1970, no. 42.

6. Beach 'Painting at Devgarh', fig. 24, with attribution to Bakhta. Andhare and Singh, *Deogarh Painting*, pl. VI (illustrated by a modern copy), make an attribution to Chokha's son Baijnath. Cf. also Pal and Glynn, *The sensuous line*, no. 38.

7. Harle and Topsfield, *Indian art in the Ashmolean Museum*, no. 90 (also Stronge, *A golden treasury*, fig. 12).

42

The marriage celebrations at Udaipur of Maharao Ram Singh II of Kota

Kota, Rajasthan, c.1851
Opaque watercolour with gold on cotton cloth
92.6×69.5cm

The architecture is recognisably that of the City Palace in Udaipur, and the ceremonies are those of a wedding. Maharao Ram Singh II of Kota (r.1827-65) is shown arriving on an elephant in the main palace courtyard at the lower left; he then approaches the auspiciously decorated gateway leading to the Zenana Mahal (seen on the left), where Maharana Sarup Singh of Mewar (r.1842-61; also with aureole) stands on a low terrace awaiting him.

The painting is in the style of Kota State, although the artist could well have travelled to Udaipur to make a preliminary record of the scene. Few events of Ram Singh II's life seem to have escaped the eyes of his artists.[1] The illustration provides information concerning an event important to Kota history. Ram Singh II was only the second Kota Maharao to marry into the family of the Maharanas of Udaipur, the most prestigious of all Rajput ruling families. He arrived in Udaipur on 9 March 1851, and married Phulkunvar Bai, sister of Maharana Sarup Singh, that same day. As reported in a contemporary chronicle, it was an occasion of great pomp and tumult. Earlier, however, Ram Singh had accepted demands made by Sarup Singh to assure the future status of the queen and any male children.[2] Ram Singh departed Udaipur a week later.

Despite the historical and documentary character of the scene, at which the events and attendants are all clearly described, the artist has introduced allusions to more private activities. The two men at the centre of the right margin, for example, look back and out of the frame; one makes a gesture of approval to an unseen person, the other receives a message or a gift from a woman who is visible only as a hand and a skirt hem.

MCB

1. For a discussion of Ram Singh II as a patron and other works from his reign, see Desai, *Life at court*, pp.116-121; Bautze, 'Portraitmalerei'.

2. Shyamaldas, *Vir Vinod*, II, pp. 1944-45. For this and other historical information given here, I am very grateful to Andrew Topsfield, who has also suggested that the portrait that must presumably show Sarup Singh – the aureoled figure on the terrace outside the palace- must have been made at Kota, for it is inaccurate; the ruler actually sported a beard at the time. For a further account of the event, with an incorrect date, see Somani, *Later Mewar*, pp.216-17.

Bibliography

Abdu'l Qadir ibn-i Muluk Shah, al-Badaoni, *Muntakhabat ut-Tawarikh*, tr. W. Haig, repr. Patna, 1973.

Abu'l Fazl Allami, *'Ain-i Akbari*, tr. H. Blochmann, Calcutta, 1938-39.

Aijazuddin, F.S., *Pahari paintings and Sikh portraits in the Lahore Museum,* London, 1977.

Andhare, S., 'Painting from the thikana of Deogarh', *Bulletin of the Prince of Wales Museum*, 10, 1967, pp.43-53.
Chronology of Mewar painting, Delhi, 1987.
and N. Singh, *Deogarh painting*, rev. ed., New Delhi, 1983.

W.G. Archer, *Indian paintings from Rajasthan*, London, 1957.
Indian miniatures, London, 1960.
Indian paintings from the Punjab Hills, 2 vols., London, 1973.
Visions of courtly India, Washington, 1976.

Arts Council, *In the image of man*, London, 1982.

Ashton, Sir Leigh, ed., *The art of India and Pakistan*, London, 1950.

Barrett, D. and B. Gray, *Painting of India*, Geneva, 1963.

J. Bautze, 'Eine Garudastandarte aus Kota im Linden-Museum', *Tribus*, Stuttgart, 1986, pp.57-82.
'Portraits of Rao Ratan and Madho Singh Hara', *Berliner Indologische Studien*, 2, 1986, pp.87-106.
'A contemporary and inscribed portrait of Jagat Singh of Kota', *Deyadharma: Studies in memory of D.C. Sircar*, ed. G. Bhattacharya, Delhi, 1986, pp.47-64.
Indian miniature paintings, c.1590-c.1850, Amsterdam, 1987.
'Zur Darstellung der Hauptgottheiten Kotas in der Malerei der zweiten Hälfte des 18. und der ersten Hälfte des 19. Jahrhunderts', *Berliner Indologische Studien*, 3, 1987, pp.253-78.
'Maharana Sangram Singh of Udaipur entertaining members of the Dutch East India Company led by Johan Josua Ketelaar', *Bulletin van het Rijksmuseum*, Amsterdam, vol. 36, 2, 1988, pp.117-32.
'Portraitmalerei unter Maharao Ram Singh von Kota', *Artibus Asiae*, XLIX, 3/4, 1988-89, pp.316-50.

Bayly, C.A., ed., *The Raj: India and the British 1600-1947*, London, 1990.

Beach, M.C., 'Painting at Devgarh', *Archives of Asian Art*, XXIV, 1970-71, pp.23-35.
Rajput painting at Bundi and Kota, Ascona, 1974.
The Grand Mogul: Imperial painting in India 1600-1660, Williamstown, Mass., 1978.
The imperial image: Paintings for the Mughal court, Washington, D.C., 1981.
The art of India and Pakistan, Durham, N.C., 1985.
Early Mughal painting, Cambridge, Mass., 1987.

Bibliothèque Nationale, *A la cour du Grand Moghol*, Paris, 1986.

Binney, E., *Panorama de la miniatura de la India*, Monterrey, 1979.

Brand, M. and G.D. Lowry, *Akbar's India: Art from the Mughal City of Victory*, New York, 1985.

British Museum, *Paintings from the Muslim courts of India*, London, 1976.

van Buitenen, J. tr., *The Mahabharata*, vol. 2, Chicago, 1975.

Chandra, P., 'A series of *Ramayana* paintings', *Bulletin of the Prince of Wales Museum*, 6, 1957-59, pp.64-70.

Chandramani, 'On Mandi paintings', *Chhavi-2*, ed. A. Krishna, Benares, 1981, pp.206-11.

Cimino, R.M. et al., *Life at court in Rajasthan*, Florence, 1985.

Colnaghi & Co., *Indian painting: Mughal and Rajput, and a Sultanate manuscript*, London, 1978.

Coomaraswamy, A.K., *Rajput painting*, 2 vols., London, 1916.
Catalogue of the Indian collections: Museum of Fine Arts, Boston, vol. 5, Cambridge, Mass., 1926.

Craven, R.C. Jr., ed., *Ramayana: Pahari paintings*, Bombay, 1990.

Crill, R., 'The Rajput courts', *The arts of India 1550-1850*, eds. J. Guy and D. Swallow, London, 1990.

Dahmen-Dallapiccola, A.L., *Ragamala-Miniaturen von 1745 bis 1700*, Wiesbaden, 1975.

Das, A.K., 'An introductory note on the Emperor Akbar's *Ramayana* and its miniatures', *Facets of Indian art*, eds. R. Skelton et al., London, 1986, pp.94-104.

Davidson, J.L., *Art of the Indian subcontinent from Los Angeles collections*, Los Angeles, 1968.

Desai, V., *Life at court: Art for India's rulers, 16th-19th centuries*, Boston, 1986.

Digby, S., 'A corpus of "Mughal" glass', *Bulletin of the School of Oriental and African Studies*, XXXVI, 1, 1973, pp.80-96.

Doshi, S. ed., *Pageant of Indian art: Festival of India in Great Britain*, Bombay, 1983.

Eastwick, E.B. tr., *The Anvar-i Suhaili or the Lights of Canopus*, Hertford, 1854.

Ebeling, K., *Ragamala painting*, Basel, 1973.

Ehnbom, D.J., *Indian miniatures: The Ehrenfeld collection*, New York, 1985.

Fondation Custodia, *L'Inde des légendes et des réalités: Miniatures indiennes et persanes de la Fondation Custodia (Collections Frits Lugt)*, Paris, 1986.

Gahlot, J.S., *Rajputane ka itihas*, vol. 1, Jodhpur, 1937.

Gangoly, O.C., *Exhibition of Indian paintings chiefly of the Jaipur school*, Calcutta, 1930.

Glück, H., *Die indischen Miniaturen des Hämzä-Romanes im Österreichischen Museum für Kunst und Industrie in Wien und in anderen Sammlungen*, Vienna, 1925.

Glynn, C., 'Seven inscribed Pahari portraits', *Los Angeles County Museum of Art Bulletin*, XXV, 1979, pp.38-55.
'Early painting in Mandi', *Artibus Asiae*, XLIV, 1, 1983, pp.21-64.

Goetz, H., 'The Nagaur school of Rajput painting', *Artibus Asiae*, XII, 1949, pp.89-98.
The art and architecture of Bikaner State, Oxford, 1950.

Gorakhshkar, S. et al., *Skönhetens Spegel*, Stockholm, 1987.

Goswamy, B.N., *Essence of Indian art*, San Francisco, 1986.
'Essence and appearance: Some notes on Indian portraiture', *Facets of Indian art*, eds. R. Skelton et al., London, 1986.
and E. Fischer, *Pahari-Meister*, Zürich, 1990.

Gray, B., 'A new Mughal painting on stuff', *Ars Islamica*, IV, 1937, pp.459-61.

Grube, E., *Muslim miniature paintings*, Venice, 1962.
Islamic paintings from the 11th to the 18th century in the collection of Hans P. Kraus, New York, n.d.

Gupta, K.S., *Mewar and the Maratha relations*, New Delhi, 1971.

Harle, J.C., and A. Topsfield, *Indian art in the Ashmolean Museum*, Oxford, 1987.

Heeramaneck, A.N., *Masterpieces of Indian painting*, n.p., 1984.

Hickmann, R. and V. Enderlein, *Indische Albumblätter: Miniaturen und Kalligraphien aus der Zeit der Moghul-Kaiser,* Leipzig, 1979.
Hodgkin, H., and T. McInerney, *Indian drawing,* London, 1983.
Ibrahim Adil Shah, *Kitab-i Nauras,* ed. N. Ahmad, New Delhi, 1956.
Inayat Khan, *The Shah Jahan Nama,* eds. W. Begley and Z.A. Desai, New Delhi, 1990.
Irwin, J.C., and M. Hall, *Indian painted and printed fabrics,* Ahmedabad, 1971.
Jahangir, *The Tuzuk-i Jahangiri, or Memoirs of Jahangir,* tr. A. Rogers and H. Beveridge, repr. London, 1968.
Jain-Neubauer, J., *The Ramayana in Pahari miniature painting,* Ahmedabad, 1981.
Khandalavala, K., *Pahari miniature painting,* Bombay, 1958.
'Two Bikaner paintings in the N.C. Mehta collection and the problem of Mandi school', *Chhavi-2,* ed. A. Krishna, Benares, 1981, pp.301-4.
Pahari miniature paintings in the N.C. Mehta collection, Ahmedabad, n.d.
and S. Doshi, *A collector's dream,* Bombay, 1987.
and M. Chandra and P. Chandra, *Miniature paintings from the Sri Motichand Khajanchi collection,* New Delhi, 1960.
Kramrisch, S., *Manifestations of Shiva,* Philadelphia, 1981.
Painted delight, Philadelphia, 1986.
Krishnadasa, R., 'A fable book for Akbar', *Times of India Annual 1966,* pp.31-40.
Leach, L., *Indian miniature paintings and drawings: The Cleveland Museum of Art,* Cleveland, 1986.
Lee, S.E., *Rajput painting,* New York, 1960.
Losty, J.P., *Indian paintings in the British Library,* New Delhi, 1986.
Malcolm, Sir John, *A memoir of Central India,* London, 1832; repr. Shannon, 1972.
Manucci, N., *Storia do Mogor,* tr. W. Irvine, Calcutta, 1907-09.
Martin, F.R., *Miniature paintings and painters of Persia, India and Turkey,* London, 1912.
Mathur, J.L., *Brij-bavani,* Sawar, 1977.
Mathur, T.K., *Feudal polity in Mewar,* Jaipur, 1987.
McInerney, T., *Indian painting 1525-1825,* London, 1982.
Mittal, J., *Indian drawings: 16th-19th century,* New Delhi, 1989.
Pal, P., *The classical tradition in Rajput painting,* New York, 1978.
and C. Glynn, *The sensuous line: Indian drawings from the Paul F. Walter collection,* Los Angeles, 1976.
et al., *Romance of the Taj Mahal,* Los Angeles, 1989.
Pasricha, I., 'Painting at Sawar and at Isarda in the 17th century', *Oriental Art,* XXVIII, 3, 1982, pp.257-69.
Patnaik, N., *A second paradise,* New York, 1985.
Rajasthan Lalit Kala Akadami, *Varsika '63,* Jaipur, 1963.
Ray, N., *Mughal court painting,* Calcutta, 1975.
Roe, Sir Thomas, *The Embassy of Sir Thomas Roe to India, 1615-1619,* ed. W. Foster, London, 1899.
Sarkar, J.N., *History of Aurangzeb,* Calcutta, 1924.
Seyller, J., 'Model and copy: The illustration of three *Razmnama* manuscripts', *Archives of Asian Art,* XVIII, 1985, pp.37-66.
Shah Nawaz Khan, *Maathir ul-Umara,* tr. H. Beveridge, Calcutta, 1911-14.
Sharma, O.P., *Indian miniature painting,* Brussels, *1974.*
Shastri, H.P. tr., *The Ramayana of Valmiki,* London, 1957.

Shukla, Y.K., *Wall paintings of Rajasthan,* Ahmedabad, 1980.
Shyam, R., *Life and times of Malik Ambar,* Delhi, 1968.
Shyamaldas, Kaviraja, *Vir vinod,* 2 vols, Udaipur, 1866, repr. in 4 vols., Delhi, 1986.
Singh, M.K. Brijraj, *The kingdom that was Kotah,* New Delhi, 1985
Singh, Kumar Sangram, *Catalogue of Indian miniature paintings (Collection of Kumar Sangram Singh of Nawalgarh),* (cyclostyle) Jaipur, 1965.
Skelton, R., *Indian miniatures from the XVth to XIXth centuries,* Venice, 1961.
Smart, E.S. and D. S. Walker, *Pride of the princes: Indian art of the Mughal era in the Cincinnati Art Museum,* Cincinnati, 1985.
Somani, R.V., *Later Mewar,* Gangapur, 1985.
Spink, W., *Krishnamandala,* Ann Arbor, 1971.
Spink and Son, *Indian miniature painting,* London, 1987.
Stronge, S. et al., *A golden treasury: Jewellery from the Indian subcontinent,* London, 1988.
Suleiman, H., *Miniatures of Babur-nama,* [Russian] Tashkent, 1970.
Tamaskar, B.G., *Malik Ambar,* Delhi, 1978.
Tandan, R.K., *Pahari ragamalas,* Bangalore, 1983.
Tillotson, G.H.R., *The Rajput palaces,* New Haven, 1987.
Tod, J., *Annals and antiquities of Rajasthan,* ed. W. Crooke, London, 1920; repr. Delhi, 1971.
Topsfield, A., *Paintings from Rajasthan in the National Gallery of Victoria,* Melbourne, 1980.
'Painting for the Rajput courts', *The arts of India,* ed. B. Gray, Oxford, 1981, pp.159-76.
An introduction to Indian court painting, London, 1984.
'Ketelaar's embassy and the *farangi* theme in the art of Udaipur', *Oriental Art,* XXX, 4, 1984, pp.350-67.
'Udaipur paintings of the Raslila', *Art Bulletin of Victoria,* 28, 1987, pp.54-70.
The City Palace Museum, Udaipur: Paintings of Mewar court life, Ahmedabad, 1990.
Tyulayev, S., *Miniatures of Babur-nama,* [Russian] Moscow, 1960.
Victoria & Albert Museum, *The Indian heritage: Court life and arts under Mughal rule,* London, 1982.
Verma, D.C., *History of Bijapur,* New Delhi, 1974.
Waldschmidt, E. and R. L., *Miniatures of musical inspiration,* vol. 2, Berlin, 1975.
Weber, R., *Porträts und historische Darstellungen in der Miniaturensammlung des Museums für Indische Kunst, Berlin,* Berlin, 1982.
Welch, S.C., *The art of Mughal India,* New York, 1963.
A flower from every meadow, New York, 1973.
Indian drawings and painted sketches, New York, 1976.
India: Art and culture 1300-1900, New York, 1985.
and M.C. Beach, *Gods, thrones and peacocks,* New York, 1965.
Wilkinson J.V.S., *The Lights of Canopus,* London, 1929.
Zebrowski, M., *Deccani painting,* London, 1983.
'Transformations in seventeenth century Deccani painting at Bijapur', *Chhavi-2,* ed. A. Krishna, Benares, 1981.